BR DIARY 1958-1967

Below:
From the age of steam . . . A typical scene of the steam age as a local headed by a Standard Class 4MT No 80152, built at Brighton a few years previously, leaves the single track of the line from Three Bridges at Ashurst Junction in 1960. The token is being surrendered to the signalman. *G. S. Robinson*

BR DIARY 1958-1967

LONDON
IAN ALLAN LTD

John Glover

Below:
To the diesel age . . . In a scene which today seems almost as dated as that of the steam picture on the preceding page, 'Western' class diesel-hydraulic No D1007 *Western Talisman* leaves Shrewsbury for Birkenhead, whilst on the right is 'Warship' No D858 *Valorous* with a Plymouth-Manchester train. The date is 1 August 1962. *P. J. Lynch*

First published 1987

ISBN 0 7110 1715 8

Published by Ian Allan Ltd, Shepperton, Surrey; and printed by Ian Allan Printing Ltd at their works at Coombelands in Runnymede, England

Front cover:
Built as a contender for the BR Type 4 power class, No D0280 *Falcon* was constructed by Brush in 1961. It is seen here at King's Cross with the down 'Master Cutler' in the early 1960s.
T. J. Edgington/Colour-Rail

The Western Region poster shows a 'Western' class diesel.
National Railway Museum, York

Contents

Preface 6

1958

The Pilot Scheme Diesels 8
The Bluebell Railway 10
Timetable Highlights 12
The Railbuses 14

1959

Reappraisal 20
Midland & Great Northern Closure 22
The AC Electric Locos 24
Diesel Unit Success 26

1960

The Guillebaud Pay Inquiry 32
Blue Pullmans 34
The Select Committee 36
Glasgow Debacle 38

1961

A New Chairman 44
The Wisdom of Dieselisation 46
The Riding of Coaches 48
The 'Deltics' 50

1962

Commercial Freedom 56
Kent Coast Electrification Complete 58
The Railway Workshops 60
Boundary Changes 62

1963

The Reshaping of British Railways 68
Passenger Services Improve 70
The Roadrailer Episode 72
The Oil Contracts 74

1964

XP64 80
Derby Research 82
Cartic 84
Merry-go-Round 86

1965

Corporate Identity 92
The Trunk Routes Report 94
Electric Transmission versus Hydraulic 96
Freightliners, but no Open Terminals 98

1966

Electrics at Euston 104
The London Peak Problem 107
The Basic Railway 110
Wagon Design 112

1967

Labour Transport Policy 118
Bournemouth Electrification 120
The Ultimate Type 4? 122
Salisbury-Exeter Singling 124

Appendices

Railway Traffic, Operations and Staff, 1958-67 127
Railway Assets as at 1 January 1958-68 128

Preface

The decade under review saw sweeping changes in British Railways. As Chairman of the British Transport Commission until mid-1961, Sir Brian Robertson's outstanding achievement was to secure previously undreamed of funds for modernisation and re-equipment. Alas, that money was not always wisely spent, and too optimistic a view was taken of traffic trends and labour costs. The Ernest Marples/Richard Beeching era which followed set about a rationalisation exercise (OED definition: 'reform an industry by eliminating waste in labour, time and materials'). And whilst from the perspective of the 1980s the Beeching action was undoubtedly necessary, positive rethinking of the railway role was notably lacking, or at least underplayed. It was left to career railwaymen like Gerard Fiennes to provide the stimulus of new ideas, of which Merry-go-Round (MGR) coal for power stations was an outstanding example. The deficit though refused to diminish permanently, despite having eased for a couple of years. The incoming Labour Government eventually appointed the redoubtable Mrs Barbara Castle as Minister of Transport, and sweeping changes were foreshadowed in what became the Transport Act 1968.

On the ground, the railway changed out of all recognition. Steam traction passed from pre-eminence to near extinction, the staff were reduced in number by over 40%, whilst the mileage of route and the number of stations and depots were cut drastically. Given the state of the economy, passenger traffic remained reasonably buoyant although freight fell away rather more. The running of express services at 100mph at last became a regular daily occurrence. During the period there were a few well publicised technical failures, and both the decisions on substitution of electric for steam train heating and of air brakes for vacuum brakes were delayed far beyond when they should have been.

In this volume I have set out some of the episodes in the progress of the British Railways of 1958 to the British Rail of 1967, which I hope reveal something of the flavour of the era. Material has been gleaned from many sources, but particularly the Annual Report and Accounts of the BTC and later the BRB, *Modern Railways*, and its predecessor *Trains Illustrated*. I am most grateful for the help I have received in the compilation of this book, especially from Geoffrey (Mr Twig) Robinson, who kindly allowed me the use of his own photographs and those of his father, Mr G. S. Robinson. Both Martin Higginson and John Phillips proved to be hoarders of extensive collections of publicity matter, some of which has been reproduced. To them and the photographers whose names appear in the credits, many thanks.

John Glover
Ewell, Surrey
July 1986

1958

'Double manning will apply to diesel and electric locomotives on passenger trains where it is necessary to employ a second man to attend to the steam heating apparatus' — BTC/ASLEF/NUR agreement.

Right:
The restoration of the record breaker *City of Truro* to traffic gladdened many hearts. The 4-4-0 was to be found working special trains all over the system, but also undertook spells in ordinary traffic. It was photographed here, appropriately, at Truro.
G. S. Robinson

The Pilot Scheme Diesels

The initial 'pilot scheme' programme of construction of 174 main line diesel locomotives was an early approval under the Modernisation Plan. In order to give the maximum experience of the various hardware on offer (and also to satisfy the domestic locomotive manufacturing industry), 14 different designs were commissioned. Within these, no less than seven makes of engine, eight types of transmission (both electric and hydraulic), and seven locomotive builders were involved. Whilst some designs of European origin were acceptable, the obvious step of purchasing some locomotives from that bastion of diesel power, the United States, was discarded for political reasons. Three years was to be allowed for evaluation before placing bulk orders and dieselising the country an area at a time, but the financial need to eliminate steam traction at the earliest opportunity quickly overtook these good intentions. The results were predictably unsatisfactory, especially as maintenance facilities and crew training barely kept up with the ensuing rush of deliveries from the manufacturers.

The engineers never really had a chance. In charting the way forward, reliability was seen as the most important attribute, and standardisation an important goal. However, the quantities of locomotives now being demanded were beyond the manufacturing capacity of any one supplier of power equipment; in any event, who was to say at this stage which designs were satisfactory and which were not? Even the numbers required of each power group of locomotives were originally down to be determined by service testing. Consequently, a large number of designs made it through to the production stage, and for which substantial orders were given. Wisely, though, there was a preponderance of English Electric designs (the only UK manufacturer with really extensive experience), and Sulzer-engined locomotives which used a well tried and tested power unit. As Appendix 1 shows, 82 main line diesels were delivered in 1958, after which the programme quickly accelerated with around 400 more being delivered each year until

Below:
The first 20 BRCW Type 2 diesels were sent to Finsbury Park where they were later joined by Nos D5330-5. All were subsequently despatched to Scotland; No D5313 was pictured at King's Cross on 3 October 1959. *John Glover*

Below right:
The North British Type 2s had an undistinguished career; some, including No D6107 pictured here, were later given a Paxman Ventura engine to replace the original NBL/MAN product. After a spell in East Anglia, this class too went north of the Border.
John Glover

The Pilot Scheme Orders

Original No series	*No of locos ordered*	*Main contractor*	*Engine manufacturer*	*bhp*	*Wheel arrangement*	*BR 1968 class No*
Type C locomotives (2,000hp+)						
D1-10	10	BR Derby	Sulzer	2,300	1Co-Co1	44
D200-9	10	English Electric	English Electric	2,000	1Co-Co1	40
D600-4	5	North British	MAN	2,000	A1A-A1A	41*
D800-2	3	BR Swindon	Maybach	2,000	B-B	42
*Not actually allocated as locomotives were withdrawn before scheme implemented.						
Type B locomotives (1,000-1,250hp)						
D5000-19	20	BR Derby	Sulzer	1,160	Bo-Bo	24
D5300-19	20	Birmingham RC&W	Sulzer	1,160	Bo-Bo	26
D5500-19	20	Brush	Mirrlees	1,250	A1A-A1A	30
D5700-19	20	Metro-Vickers	Crossley	1,200	Co-Bo	28
D5900-9	10	English Electric	English Electric	1,100	Bo-Bo	23
D6100-9	10	North British	MAN	1,000	Bo-Bo	21
D6300-5	6	North British	MAN	1,000	B-B	22
Type A locomotives (600-1,000hp)						
D8000-19	20	English Electric	English Electric	1,000	Bo-Bo	20
D8200-9	10	BTH	Davey Paxman	800	Bo-Bo	15
D8400-9	10	North British	Davey Paxman	800	Bo-Bo	16
Total ordered	174					

the mid-1960s. Standardisation became a lost cause for a whole generation of locomotives.

The pilot scheme prototypes were delivered from 1957 to 1959, with the majority appearing in 1958. Even where full preparation had been made for their reception, the number of designs which individuals had to be conversant with was bewildering. At the newly opened Finsbury Park diesel depot on the Eastern Region, for instance, eight different classes were allocated in the first few years, including no less than five different Type B locomotives (later, Type 2).

Left:
The BR/Sulzer Type 2s found themselves in the King's Cross area due to their acceptability to the Southern Region on cross-London transfer freight workings. No D5052 leaves Oakleigh Park with a New Barnet-bound local. Note the steam style shed plate on the gangway doors. *John Glover*

The Bluebell Railway

The Bluebell Railway in Sussex first sprang to public attention in 1956, when Miss Bessemer of Chailey forced the reintroduction of passenger services between East Grinstead and Lewes. Previously closed in 1955, Miss Bessemer secured the running of four trains per day each way from 7 August 1956, after finding that the legal requirements for the discontinuation of passenger services had not been observed.

The service which British Railways offered was merely that which was required by the original Act of Parliament; the trains called only at West Hoathly, Horsted Keynes, Sheffield Park and Newick & Chailey, as the other two stations (Kingscote and Barcombe) were not mentioned in the Act. Signalling, already dismantled, was not reinstated, and trains were confined to the single line without the benefit of passing loops. There was no through ticketing to other parts of the system, and local opinion, rightly or wrongly, was that British Railways having been caught out were now complying with the law with bad grace.

Not that the traffic offering did anything to deny the validity of the closure proposal. The crowds which gathered to see the reopening quickly melted away, and a single coach hauled by a veteran LB&SCR locomotive was more than adequate. The closure process started again, and this time there were no mistakes. Services ceased from 17 March 1958, apart from Horsted Keynes station where the electrified service to Haywards Heath and Seaford continued throughout until it too was withdrawn in 1963.

Below:
During the period of 'sulky service' between reopening in 1956 and final closure under BR, a single coach sufficed for the four trains each way daily. Class E4 0-6-2T No 32508 takes over the train from a 'C2X' at East Grinstead in 1958.
G. S. Robinson

Left:
All signalling had been removed after the line closed for the first time; when reopened trains were restricted to a single line. A footplate view from the south at the approach to a silent Sheffield Park shows the rust on the disused rails.
G. S. Robinson

Such however had been the public interest aroused that a further development took place, which eventually brought a five-mile stretch of the line more traffic than at any time in its previous history. The Bluebell Railway Preservation Society was formed, and on 7 August 1960 ran its first train in the midst of the beautiful Sussex countryside between Sheffield Park and a site just short of Horsted Keynes. Later, entry to Horsted Keynes station was negotiated, and the whole is now Bluebell Railway property. The BRPS was the first voluntary body to operate a regular steam passenger service on a standard gauge railway; their five millionth passenger was carried in 1983.

Left:
There was no need to hurry, with a generous time of 45min or so allowed for the journey. The train crew wait patiently for their photographing passenger at Newick & Chailey on 14 March 1958. The train, headed by 'C2X' class 0-6-0 No 32440, had been stopped specially in the open beyond the canopy. *G. S. Robinson*

Below:
The closure notice, showing all services to be withdrawn from 17 March.

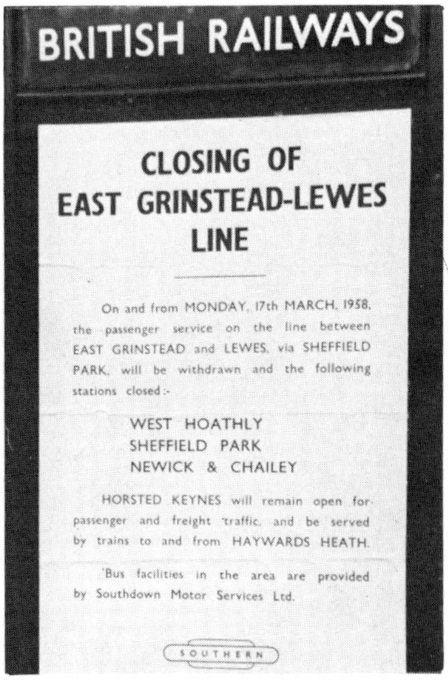

BRITISH RAILWAYS

CLOSING OF
EAST GRINSTEAD-LEWES
LINE

On and from MONDAY, 17th MARCH, 1958, the passenger service on the line between EAST GRINSTEAD and LEWES, via SHEFFIELD PARK, will be withdrawn and the following stations closed:-

WEST HOATHLY
SHEFFIELD PARK
NEWICK & CHAILEY

HORSTED KEYNES will remain open for passenger and freight traffic, and be served by trains to and from HAYWARDS HEATH.

'Bus facilities in the area are provided by Southdown Motor Services Ltd.

SOUTHERN

Timetable Highlights

The timetables of 1958 showed that the railway was beginning to change. Smart new multiple-units were providing much improved services on an increasing number of lines, while steam traction on the trunk routes was reaching its postwar zenith. 1939 standards were still not being matched regarding fastest journey times, but the average speed of services showed marked accelerations.

One noticeable feature was the lack of early morning business services, especially from London. The London Midland Region bravely introduced the 'Caledonian' from Euston at 7.45am which, after stops at Crewe and Carlisle, was due into Glasgow Central at 2.30pm, thus beating the 7.50am 'Fair Maid' from King's Cross to Edinburgh by one minute. This train ran for the summer period only, which was just as well for travellers on the 8.40am from Manchester. Pathing difficulties meant that their through coaches were detained at Carstairs no less than 46min, awaiting the 8.57am from Liverpool.

The speed record passed briefly from the Western Region to the North Eastern when the 5.5pm Newcastle to King's Cross was timed to cover the 44.1 miles from Darlington to York in 39min at an average 67.8mph, thus beating the 'Bristolian' by 0.2mph. September saw the Western Region recover its title with the 1.50pm Bristol to Paddington. A stop at Reading was inserted into the schedule to replace a slip coach, and the train was booked to cover the 41.3 miles from Swindon to Reading in 36min at 68.8mph. Simultaneously, the NE eased its 39min timing to 40min.

September also saw the introduction of the 'Master Cutler', a

Below:
The 'Master Cutler' was for a time the exclusive preserve of the newly delivered English Electric Type 4s; five of the first batch were sent to the Great Northern. No D208 passes Peterborough North with the up morning service from Sheffield Victoria.
Dennis C. Ovenden

diesel-hauled Pullman on the Great Northern line to Sheffield via Retford and initially with a 2hr 45min timing. Even so, the 7.50am from Sheffield Victoria achieved a timing 52min superior to that of its Marylebone-bound predecessor. This service demonstrated better rolling stock utilisation, as the train made a midday return trip to Sheffield before returning from King's Cross at 7.20pm. Like the improved services to Norwich being offered by the Great Eastern, this was made possible by the delivery of the first 10 English Electric Type 4 diesels. On the GE, the 'Britannias' were displaced to Essex coast services with great effect, a best effort being 86min for the 5.27pm Liverpool Street to Clacton, including two stops.

By the autumn, electrification was adding up to 20min recovery time into Euston services, which by default gave the Western the four fastest Birmingham services between Paddington and Snow Hill. Two hours dead was the best timing. On a brighter note, six trains per day formed of Cross-Country diesel sets were introduced on the Birmingham-Hereford-Cardiff route, cutting journey times to 3hr 15min, an improvement of up to 40min.

On the branches, Fort William-Mallaig was granted a summer Sunday service for the first time. The two trains in each direction both carried an observation car. Closure of the Whitby-Loftus line in the northeast brought vast traffic to the single line from Middlesbrough via Battersby, with a remarkable 15 southbound and 14 northbound trains worked entirely by diesel units.

Economies on the Southern in the autumn closed Cannon Street during the midday off-peak period and after 10.15pm; the station was closed from 3.15pm on Saturdays and all day Sundays. Some suburban services were cut in frequency, but the recently introduced Hastings diesel service was unaltered.

Below:
Hastings line diesel-electric multiple-units Nos 1018 and 1016 leaving Tonbridge with a Charing Cross-Hastings service on 12 April 1958.
J. N. Faulkner

The Railbuses

The BTC wanted to introduce a vehicle which would be more economical even than a single unit DMU as used experimentally on the Buckingham-Banbury branch in 1957. In that case, traffic was attracted, but the earnings still fell well short of direct costs. Looking for a maximum economy vehicle, the Commission placed orders for 22 lightweight four-wheeled railbuses. The cost was about three times that of a bus with similar capacity, and it was hoped to reduce running costs to 3s (15p) per mile. Use was to be on rural branch lines.

Quite why so many different designs were necessary merely to try out a concept is unclear, but as the table shows a considerable degree of latitude was allowed to the individual contractors within overall dimensional and performance specifications. Internally, the vehicles resembled conventional DMUs; the riding qualities (of the Park Royal vehicle) were described by *Trains Illustrated*:

'On straight track the riding was good for a four-wheeler, though the rubber suspension gave the body a good bounce at times, but even at slow speeds the long wheelbase and light weight of the vehicle made the negotiation of pointwork fairly lively for the passenger'.

Operationally, some experimentation took place. After securing union agreement for the guard to act also as a ticket collector, and the fitting of retractable steps, the number of stopping places was increased. On the Crieff-Comrie branch of the Scottish Region for instance, passengers were picked up and set down at Strageath and Pittenzie level crossings, whereas on the Audley End-Bartlow branch of the Eastern Region the staff were authorised to organise extra off-peak journeys according to demand. Indeed, large

Below:
One of the best known of the railbus types was that of AC Cars. No W79977 has just arrived from Cirencester, and is providing a connection at Kemble into the 9.04am 'Cheltenham Spa Express'.
P. J. Sharpe

numbers of passengers were an embarrassment, as there was no way in which a railbus working could be strengthened, and additional journeys were the only answer. On an occasion, 110 passengers were recorded on one railbus, way in excess of the nominal carrying capacity.

Another disadvantage was the inability to carry bulky luggage, bicycles or prams, but on the technical side the lightweight railbuses could not be relied upon to operate the signalling track circuits, a substantial snag. Perhaps the greatest exponent of railbus potential was the Western Region, whose Kemble-Tetbury and Kemble-Cirencester services were thus worked from 2 February 1959. New ground level sleeper-built halts were opened, derelict stations restored, and the timetables much improved; nevertheless one wonders at the opening of the halt at Trouble House, when the only habitation in the area was the 17th century inn of the same name!

The railbuses disappeared in the 1960s, after Beeching demonstrated that even if they ran packed to the gunwales all the time there were still not nearly enough passengers to justify the provision of a rail service. A few, notably the German-built machines, survived into preservation.

British Railways Railbuses

Builder	*Dimensions*	*Weight*	*Seats*	*bhp*	*No*	*Vehicle Nos*
Bristol/ECW	42ft 4in×9ft 3in	13½t	56	112	2	Sc79958/9
Waggon und Maschinenbau	41ft 10in×8ft 8in	15t	56	150	5	E79960-4
D. Wickham & Co	38ft 0in×9ft 0in	11¼t	44	105	5	Sc79965-9
Park Royal Vehicles	42ft 0in×9ft 3in	15t	50	150	5	M/Sc79970-4
A C Cars Ltd	36ft 0in×8ft 11in	14t	46	150	5	W/Sc79975-9

Above left:
One of the pair of railbuses with Eastern Coach Works bodies is seen during construction at Lowestoft in 1958 before being lowered on to the Bristol-built underframe. *BR*

Above:
A Waggon und Maschinenbau railbus poses over the pits in the new Cambridge multiple-unit maintenance depot on 5 March 1959. The Eastern Region was in the forefront of providing adequate facilities for the new traction. *BR*

1958

Right:
Automatic Warning Control was being installed at an increasing rate. The standard BR system was in operation between Euston and Blisworth, Edinburgh and Glasgow, and King's Cross and York by the end of 1958, a total of 288 route miles. 'A4' Pacific No 60007 *Sir Nigel Gresley* demonstrates its engine receiver passing over the track inductors. *BR*

Below:
'One off' special trains with remarkably poor stock utilisation were still permitted. With the sunshine coming through after a night of heavy rain, Class U1 2-6-0 No 31905 places the empty coaches of a Ramblers' excursion into the sidings at Groombridge.
G. S. Robinson

Above:
In 1958 steam still reigned supreme on the main lines. On the Western Region, Collett's 'Castle' class 4-6-0s continued in top link service. No 5055 *Earl of Eldon* awaits departure from Kingswear, with Driver F. J. Bowden at the controls of the up 'Torbay Express' on 15 September. *G. S. Robinson*

Left:
Marshalling yard modernisation proceeded apace; in East London the new Temple Mills yard was opened on 15 September. After passing over the hump and through the king points, wagons were braked in one of the two pairs of primary retarders, seen in this picture. The stated yard capacity was 4,500 wagons per day. *BR*

Above:
The North British Locomotive Co and C. A. Parsons developed a 1,750hp coal-burning gas turbine mechanical 1A1A-A1A1 locomotive under the aegis of the Ministry of Fuel and Power. It never did appear publicly, in spite of frequent forecasts of imminent completion. This model is in the Glasgow Museum of Transport. *John Glover*

Above right:
The diesel multiple-unit had yet to take over all branch services, though the signs were there. A pair of SECR push-pull units (but only one with locomotive) stand at Bexhill West on the shuttle service to Crowhurst. In the sidings on the left stands one of the new Hastings main line diesel units. *G. S. Robinson*

Right:
The Western Region and its Great Western forebear were always known for their display of notices, mostly of the 'thou shalt not' variety. At Kingswear, anybody who did not realise that the colours referred to the route availability of the larger locomotive types might have been forgiven for thinking that *Thomas, Edward, Gordon* and *James* were being singled out. *G. S. Robinson*

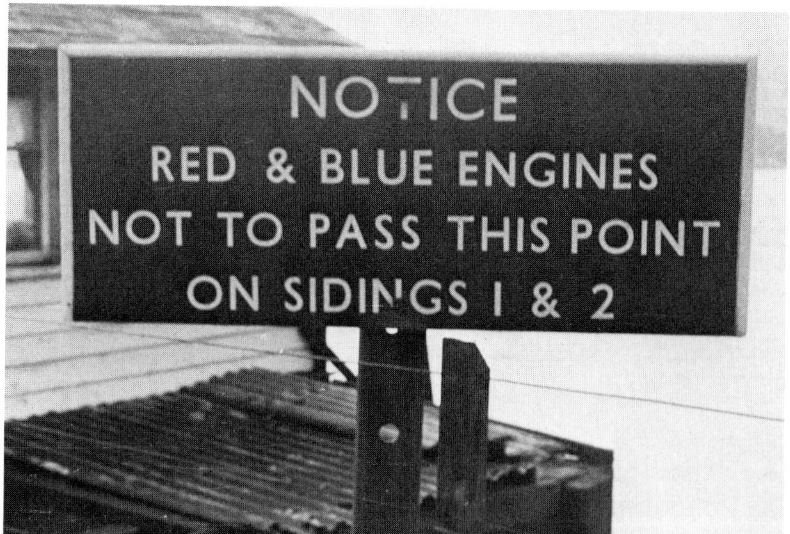

1959

'We are constantly encouraged with visions of the future, wherein faster services will be operated with astonishing economies of manpower and material, but . . . will the traffic stand another year or so of indifferent service on some trunk routes and still be there when modernisation arrives?' — *Trains Illustrated* editorial.

Right:
The Modernisation Plan provided for the concentration of freight sundries (less than wagonload) traffic. Goods are seen being unloaded on to a slat conveyor in the new Peterborough Depot on 13 July 1959; even in this official photograph a prodigious amount of manpower seems to be necessary. *BR*

Reappraisal

The deeper the BTC sank into a financial mire, with few signs that operational performance was improving, the more strident became the calls for a re-examination of the Modernisation Plan of 1955. The BTC produced their own document as a White Paper, and the 'Reappraisal' was published at the end of July. Looking forward to 1963 only, the main conclusions were:

- Modernisation must be speeded up further, as must the rationalisation of outdated facilities.
- The financial structure of the BTC with its high fixed interest charges needed to be reconsidered.
- The Modernisation Plan itself was soundly based, and there was no need for any fundamental changes.

Indeed, so confident were the BTC of the rightness of their cause that they forecast a net working surplus of £45-95 million by 1963. But, in coming to this conclusion, it was soon clear that an over-optimistic view had been taken of the ability of the modernised railway to win back traffic, and too much had been made of the general buoyancy of economic activity which was not being reflected in those rail users, the heavy industries. Likewise, good financial results for the Norwich area DMU scheme did not necessarily mean that this would be repeated everywhere. Some price increases were contemplated, particularly to counter the cost of peak provision for passengers in cities.

Turning to specific proposals, the reappraisal called for:

- Closure of 10 of the remaining 22 locomotive workshops.
- Substantial withdrawals of local passenger and goods services, and closure of about 1,800 miles of network. However, there would be no main line closures before 1963, and the Great Central and the Settle & Carlisle were specifically excluded.

Right:
One modernisation feature which was never in doubt was the replacement of the steam shunting engine with its diesel equivalent. Over 1,000 350hp shunters were built from 1953; No D3519 is seen with a GWR pattern shunter's truck.
G. S. Robinson

- Electrification resources concentrated on suburban services except for Manchester/Liverpool-Euston, thus putting off the GN main line scheme indefinitely and also the suburban scheme until 1964.
- Relative economics of hydraulic and electric transmission for diesel locomotives under study; some diesel schemes were showing rates of return as low as 5½%, others as high as 50%.
- Vacuum brake fitting of 16-ton mineral wagons held up by search for a satisfactory coupler.
- Freight traffic concentrated at fewer depots and railheads, particularly domestic coal. Meanwhile, marshalling yard rationalisation and replacement with modern yards to be accelerated.
- Installation of long welded rail to be increased to 320 route miles per year, and 3,000 more miles of route to be equipped with power signalling by 1963.
- Flyovers, to relieve bottlenecks, to be built at Hitchin, Welwyn Garden City, Retford and Rugby; additional running lines to be laid in many locations; Severn Bridge route to be developed to relieve the Severn Tunnel.
- Experiments with Automatic Half Barrier level crossings (subject to Ministry approval) and Centralised Traffic Control to be installed on the Central Wales line, York-Beverley, Honeybourne-Cheltenham and elsewhere.

Above:
Plans to make additional capacity available to and from South Wales via the Severn Bridge came to an abrupt halt when the bridge was partly destroyed after a ship was in collision with it. The 9.10am Cardiff-Bristol is seen crossing the bridge from the viewpoint of Sharpness Docks on 22 February 1959.
J. Spencer Gilks

Below:
The Great Central main line had been suspect economically for years, but 'Reappraisal' specifically excluded it from the possibility of closure for the succeeding five years. Ex-LNER Class B1 4-6-0 No 61206 heads the 6.18pm Marylebone-Sheffield Victoria between Akeman Street and Grendon Junction on 2 July 1959. *M. Mitchell*

Midland & Great Northern Closure

The Midland & Great Northern Joint Railway never had a chance. It was constructed initially by local interests, who soon found out that the serving of sparsely populated rural districts could only result in a hand-to-mouth financial existence. Consequently, offers by the Midland and Great Northern railways respectively, who saw some competitive advantages for themselves vis-à-vis the Great Eastern, were eagerly accepted. The M&GN reached its full extent of 189 route miles in 1893, by which time it was securely attached to its parent companies via Saxby, and via Peterborough and Spalding.

The line never prospered, attracting only agricultural and horticultural traffic locally, with some fish from Lowestoft and Yarmouth and timber imports at Wisbech and Lynn. In 1963 the LNER made major economies including the virtual closure of the line's workshops at Melton Constable; further cutbacks took place in 1953, after which the line was closed at night and traffic diverted to the largely parallel former Great Eastern lines. Passenger traffic boomed at summer weekends (only), when the mainly single line with passing loops was worked to capacity. Every loop was occupied with trains originating variously from points such as Chesterfield, Kettering and King's Norton, en route for the sunny delights of the East Coast seaside resorts.

Below right:
Freight traffic at Potter Heigham was being handled by ex-GER Class J17 0-6-0 No 65551, seen here from a departing passenger train.
G. S. Robinson

Below:
Perhaps the most famous landmark on the M&GN, Sutton Swing Bridge over the River Nene, was shared by road and rail; after closure, both parts were used by the road. Note the signalboxes both sides of the bridge as well as the bridge keeper's eyrie, and also the level crossing. *G. S. Robinson*

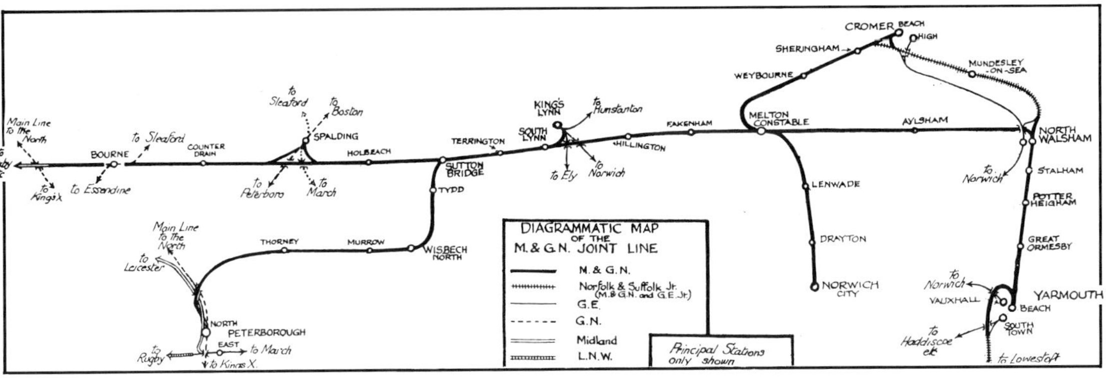

Complete closure apart from a few minor sections was put forward in 1958, and the M&GN became the largest single proposal ever considered by the Transport Users' Consultative Committees. The minimum savings were estimated at £640,000 per annum (at contemporary prices). Proposals were submitted in September 1958, and representations were received from four County Councils, one County Borough, one Borough Council, six Urban District Councils, 16 Rural District Councils and 23 Parish Councils, as well as from associations of Local Authorities, Chambers of Trade and of Commerce, many other bodies and a number of private firms and individuals. Astoundingly, by the middle of November the TUCCs had recorded their approval subject to certain minor provisos, and on 25 November the CTCC considered and confirmed the Minutes. 'This major proposal', said the BTC's Annual Report, 'was therefore dealt with in 10 weeks; and the Central Committee were good enough to congratulate all parties concerned'. Actual closure took place on 28 February 1959.

Perhaps the experience of the early 1960s when some closure somewhere was almost a weekly occurrence put a stop to such easy options, when the people as a whole became alarmed at what was going on. In these far-off days however, there was no holding back, and concentration on immediate or short-term savings was the order of the day. Timescales were reduced from 9-10 months to 8-10 weeks, and approved withdrawals of passenger services by the TUCCs rose from 28 in 1958 to 49 in 1959. Major retrenchment had begun.

Below left:
The single line of the M&GN imposed severe constraints, and a tablet exchange apparatus was used to speed operation. Ivatt 2-6-0 No 43158 on a Yarmouth-Birmingham train changes tablets at 50mph at Holbeach on 30 July 1958, while sister locomotive No 43080 awaits the road.
G. S. Robinson

Below:
There was little to do at Twenty, thus called it was said after an obscure reference on the Ordnance Survey map and the lack of any nearby settlement. Three railwaymen pass the time of day while waiting for the single line ahead to clear.
G. S. Robinson

The AC Electric Locos

For the main line electrification in progress, a single class of mixed traffic locomotives was envisaged. Rather than stipulating definitive ratings to the manufacturers, British Railways instead set down a number of duties which the locomotives must be capable of performing. Briefly, these were:

- To be capable of hauling a 475-ton passenger train from Manchester to London at a maximum speed of 100mph with an average speed of 67mph inclusive of one stop of one minute duration and running for four miles at 15mph.
- To haul a 950-ton freight over the same route at an average of 42mph. The locomotive would also need to be capable of making three consecutive starts on a 1 in 100 gradient and accelerating up to 20mph, and running for 10 miles at 10mph.

A further principal requirement was that dc traction motors and mercury-arc rectifiers be used, although it was agreed later to substitute semi-conductors on some locomotives. For the benefit of the Civil Engineer a wheel diameter of 48in was specified, and a maximum axle load of 20 tons. To reduce the unsprung weight it was decided (wisely as it was proved much later on) to use a flexible drive. The designers were also required to adopt a common cab layout, and the locomotives were to have similar handling characteristics. Vacuum train brakes and air brakes for the locomotive were provided as standard.

Given the lack of UK manufacturing experience for ac

Below:
After a career as a gas turbine locomotive, No E1000 (later E2001) was converted for further use as a crew training locomotive on the 25kV ac electrified lines between Manchester and Crewe. *BR*

Manufacturer	AEI/BTH Rugby	AEI/ Metrovick Manchester	English Electric	NBL/GEC	Doncaster/ AEI
No series	E3001-23 E3096-7	E3046-55	E3024-35 E3098-3100	E3036-45	E3056-95
Class Nos	AL1/81	AL2/82	AL3/83	AL4/84	AL5/85
No in class	25	10	15	10	40
Total weight (tons)	80.0	78.4	73.0	77.0	79.0
Length over buffers (ft)	56.5	56.0	52.5	53.5	56.5
Power (hp)	3,200	3,310	2,950	3,080	3,200

locomotives, five designs totalling 100 locomotives were ordered, to derive a satisfactory standard for future production. Originally intended for the East Coast main line as well, the intention was to have a differently geared version for freight work; this was subsequently abandoned when it became clear there would be no more electrification for the foreseeable future. External design advice was given by the Design Panel within the confines of a box-on-wheels shape; this consisted of achieving a more or less uniform frontal appearance and attention to details.

A summary of the locomotives appears in the above Table. First to emerge were the AEI/BTH locomotives, appearing towards the close of 1959. These joined the solitary Metrovick gas turbine locomotive No E2001, which had been converted to a straight electric in the previous year, and was in use for crew training and on engineers' trains. Unlike this locomotive's black livery lined out in silver, the new deliveries were turned out in a fetching shade of electric blue.

Below left:
First of the AEI/BTH production batch of locomotives, No E3001 was posed at the head of a train of wagons for photographic purposes. Although fitted out with a four-character indicator panel, there was then no clear idea as to how this was to be used. *AEI*

Below:
A low angle photograph of No E3036 emphasised the slightly more rounded styling applied to the GEC-built locomotives. Later, as Class 84, these turned out to be the first to be withdrawn.
Ian Allan Library

Diesel Unit Success

With deliveries of diesel multiple-units reaching 80% of the 4,000 planned total, interest centred on how well they were doing. Certainly, they were clean and attractive and appealing to the public, but what was the effect on patronage, and what happened to the costs of operation?

The first 'Diesel Multi-Unit' schemes were implemented in the West Riding and in West Cumberland, with sets being delivered from 1954 onwards. Thereafter progress was rapid, as may be seen from the Appendix; 1959 saw 40% of all coaching train miles in the North Eastern Region so operated. This was followed by the Eastern and Scottish Regions (25% each), with a national average of 19%. Fortunately, technical reliability was not a problem, once the maintenance arrangements had been sorted out. Some units were equipped with more powerful engines, not only to give better performance, but also to enable them to haul a parcels van. This latter was seen as an effective way of reducing lightly loaded parcels train mileage. Design variety was of course extensive, in vehicle lengths, seating density, number of cars in a unit, and provision of gangways, buffets and lavatories. Changes of mind were also apparent, as in the strengthening of the Southern's 'Hampshire' units from two to three cars by the construction of additional trailers to meet the demand.

'In all Regions and wherever the new diesel multiple-unit trains are in commission, they have on many routes completely changed the picture of travel by rail' announced the BTC grandly. The general improvement masked a wide disparity, and there were

Below:
The Southern Region pursued a policy of electric transmission for their diesel units, which offered greater compatibility with their straight electric stock. Indeed, it was even envisaged that the DMUs could later be converted to electric traction. 'Hastings' unit No 1015 takes the down platform loop at Crowhurst with a semi-fast service. *P. J. Sharpe*

hints that resources were being transferred from the less successful to those with a growing traffic. Of the 1959 schemes, Sheffield-Barnsley and Liverpool-St Helens-Wigan were singled out as achieving a tripling of revenue. These contrasted sadly with Oxford-Cambridge, Craigendoran-Arrochar and Aberdeen-Peterhead, all of which recorded less than 10% improvement. It was admitted that some of the lines converted were never expected to show first class results, and it was foreseen that services where the public did not respond would have to be abandoned.

The most remarkable growth rate was found on the first scheme of all, Bradford Exchange-Leeds Central-Harrogate-Knaresborough. Introduced in June 1954, receipts in four years climbed steadily until they reached a level five times that of the previous steam service. 'Substantial' train working economies resulted, though more units had to be drafted in to cope with the traffic, and neither prevented partial abandonment of the service in the 1960s. Spectacular revenue growth could not disguise the modest earnings for an urban service.

West Riding scheme

	Receipts	*Index*
*1954**	£23,200	100
1955	£32,200	139
1956	£50,300	217
1957	£99,000	427
1958	£116,000	500

*steam service

Above:
Messrs Cravens Ltd of Sheffield received major orders for the supply of diesel multiple-units.

Below:
A Derby Lightweight DMU set arrives at Bradford for refuelling. These units were the first of the extensive fleet built in the modernisation years. *Ian Allan Library*

1959

Above:
The *Daily Mirror* was responsible for Compound 4-4-0 No 41101 being painted at Gorton Works with a yellow boiler and tender, red cab, splashers and coupling rods, and white wheels. The locomotive was fitted with a chime whistle belonging to a 'Clan' class Pacific, and set to work on August Bank Holiday with a Manchester-Blackpool excursion. It was photographed at Newton Heath on 31 July 1959. 'Sacrilege', said *Trains Illustrated*. *J. E. Wilkinson*

Right:
It was still possible to find the mixed train in service. Ex-LBSCR 'A1X' class 'Terrier' tank No 32650 approaches Havant on the run from Hayling Island in June.
G. S. Robinson

Left:
The survivors of the Webb versions of the Ramsbottom 'Special Tanks' of 1870 were withdrawn during the year. In service locomotive stock, three of the 0-6-0STs were pictured in Wolverton Carriage Works. *G. S. Robinson*

Below:
New into traffic in 1959 were 24 2,552hp dc electric locomotives for use in Kent. Built at Doncaster Works, they were intended for freight and also on duties such as the 'Night Ferry' which loaded up to 700 tons. Livery was an adventurous malachite green with red and white lining and grey roof and window surround. *Sam Lambert*

Right:
The fleet-footed 'Schools' Class V 4-4-0s were given less exacting tasks. A polished No 30917 *Ardingly* pauses at Lewes in the evening sunshine with a London Bridge-Brighton service.
G. S. Robinson

Below:
Despite the widespread construction of diesel shunters from the early 1950s onwards, it took a long time to eliminate steam from the shunting yards despite its acknowledged shortcomings. A 1904-built North British Railway 0-6-0T No 68335 of Class J88 shunts Maryhill Coal Yard. Note the antiquated dumb buffers, which compare rather oddly with the vacuum brake.
P. J. Lynch

1960

'Anyone who travelled widely on British Railways in 1960 would notice the gradual spread of new amenities such as improved heating and sound insulation, more attractive plastic finishes and lighter fabrics, improved lighting, better ashtrays, illuminated signs outside the toilets, double glazed windows and litter baskets in corridors' — BTC Annual Report.

Below:
'Sunset and evening star . . .'. The last steam locomotive built for British Railways, Class 9F 2-10-0 No 92220, was turned out from Swindon Works in March 1960. Fittingly, perhaps, the '9Fs' were capable and efficient locomotives, although their useful life was curtailed by the end of steam traction. *BR*

The Guillebaud Pay Inquiry

The years 1955 to 1958 were marked by particular difficulties in wage negotiations because of the railways' growing financial deficits. In April 1958, pay claims for the salaried, footplate and the conciliation (ie ordinary railwaymen) grades were rejected, and the unions called for a national strike. This was averted by Government intervention, and agreement eventually reached.

Further discussion led to the setting up of the Railway Pay Committee of Inquiry under the Chairmanship of C. W. Guillebaud CBE, with its terms of reference based upon the establishment of job comparability with other industries. Reporting in March 1960, the Committee analysed a total of 153 railway grades. Although comparability was problematical, they concluded that the scales were 10% below those ruling outside British Railways for conciliation staff. However, after allowing for advantages such as relative job security and travel facilities, the Committee concluded that 8% on basic rates plus further adjustments for certain grades would be appropriate. Salaried staff

Below:
Stationmaster R. A. Neills of East Grinstead stands outside his office; the water supply is by courtesy of the Metropolitan Drinking Fountains & Cattle Troughs Association. *G. S. Robinson*

Below right:
Driver Fear and his fireman pose in the cab doorway of '57XX' class 0-6-0PT No 9629 somewhere on the Exe Valley branch. *G. S. Robinson*

were awarded 10%. Revised rates of pay were backdated to 4 January 1960.

The principle of comparability was thus established, and remained a prime union argument for many years in negotiating pay claims. The British Transport Commission, although endorsing the principle of an equitable wage, bemoaned the additional cost of the settlement at £33 million in 1960. Besides representing half of the then British Railways deficit, it also undermined the calculations embodied in the reappraisal of the previous year. Nevertheless, it eased the severe labour shortage which was causing widespread cancellation of freight trains and trip workings, particularly in the Midlands and the London area. The Select Committee on Nationalised Industries had this to say:

'The difficulty found in recruiting operating grade staff points to the change that has come over the whole employment situation on the railways since the war. Before then, a career on the railways had the great attraction of offering permanency; now, at a time of national full employment, that attraction is not so great. Furthermore, employment by British Railways is affected by another point — the fact that all men are on national wage rates. Inevitably, in some areas of the country where there are more jobs than people, local industries offer high rates of pay and the railways, with their national wage structure, are at a disadvantage'.

For the time being, anyway, Guillebaud saved the day, and in the BTC's own words 'It is right to record that the Report and its acceptance by the Government transformed the situation from one of near breakdown of the services to one of greatly improved stability and morale'.

Top:
A permanent way gang photographed during track relaying work. The sheer size of the gang is worthy of note.
G. S. Robinson

Above:
The guard of the Exe Valley train prepares to hurry the photographer on board.
G. S. Robinson

Blue Pullmans

Services between London and Manchester were diverted to the Midland route from St Pancras to Manchester Central as electrification of the former LNWR lines got under way. To sweeten the pill of extended journey times, the BTC resolved to introduce high quality business services with Pullman standards of comfort. Accordingly, two six-car first class only trains were ordered from Metro-Cammell, and these entered service on 4 July 1960. Three similar eight-car trains but with second class accommodation also were supplied to the Western Region, and these operated from September.

The trains were finished in Nanking blue with white window surrounds, thus anticipating later livery developments. External design was uncluttered, without unnecessary additions such as four-character indicator boxes. Overall appearance was very pleasing. Internally, the finish and appointments were superb. Low density seating in the first class gave only 132 seats in a six-car train on the London Midland, and the general plushy appearance was enhanced by rosewood or ebony partitions with inlaid murals. Seats were alterable to a semi-reclining position, and adjustable venetian blinds were installed between the panes of the double glazing. Table lamps supplemented fluorescent ceiling lighting, and lamps were also set in the undersides of the luggage racks above each table. Many of these features have since become standard fitments, but one facility which has not been perpetuated was the separate toilets for the two sexes.

The trains were powered by a pair of NBL/MAN 12-cylinder 1,000hp engines giving a top speed of 90mph. This enabled the 299-ton 'Midland Pullman' to offer the fastest schedule ever between London and Manchester, even allowing for the difficult nature of the Midland route north of Derby with its severe curvature and gradients each side of the 980ft Peak Forest summit

Right:
Five Blue Pullman trains were constructed by Metro-Cammell. One of the seven-car units with both first and second class accommodation for the Western Region services to Bristol and to Wolverhampton was pictured on 2 May 1960. *BR*

Left:
On occasion, failure comes to all. A 'Jinty' 0-6-0 No 47449 propels a failed 'Midland Pullman' unit into Cricklewood depot for examination and repair. *A. Swain*

which then formed the main line. The initial timetable provided the following:

'Midland Pullman' timetable from 4 July 1960

08.50 ↓	Manchester Central	↑ 21.21
09.04 ↓	Cheadle Heath	↑ 21.07
12.03 ↓	St Pancras	↑ 18.10
12.45 ↓	St Pancras	↑ 16.00
14.10 ↓	Leicester London Rd	↑ 14.33

On the Western Region, one train operated from Wolverhampton to Paddington and back, with a midday return trip to Birmingham Snow Hill, and another service made two return trips from Bristol to Paddington. The economics of all Blue Pullman services were questionable given that five train sets were required to maintain only three diagrams, but the boost they gave to the railway image at a time when it was sorely needed was undeniable. Sadly, the riding qualities of the sets were indifferent, and this problem persisted throughout the lives of the units. The last were withdrawn in 1973.

Below:
The 'Midland Pullman' in service: the up morning train from Manchester passes through Cheedale in North Derbyshire en route to St Pancras. *John Clarke*

The Select Committee

The Commission met their Waterloo in 1960 when British Railways were examined by the House of Commons Select Committee on Nationalised Industries. Although the later (unpublished) but supposedly even more critical Stedeford Committee report also had a bearing on the legislation which was to follow, the BTC visibly wilted when confronted with a searching investigation of its work. It was during the examination of witnesses that Sir James Dunnett, then Permanent Secretary to the Minister of Transport, uttered the memorable response 'I find it difficult to understand how the whole of the modernisation scheme could have the economic results forecast by the BTC in their last reappraisal', while the Treasury contented themselves by remarking acidly that the modernisation plan was 'merely a hotch-potch of the things that the Commission was saying it was desirable to try to achieve by 1970, ill qualified and not really explainable'.

Galloping bankruptcy was now staring the BTC in the face; the Select Committee's strictures cannot have made comfortable reading. The main findings were:

- The size and shape of British Railways must be such that the BTC can meet its break-even financial obligations, but this presupposes a knowledge of profitability of Regions and services, and it was clear that large expenditures on modernisation had been made with precious little regard to profitability.
- Nevertheless, the national interest may require some services to be maintained even if they are not profitable, in order to relieve the road system or to meet social considerations. Decisions in such cases should be made by the Minister, and not the Commission; the cost of providing these services should be met out of public funds, and paid openly for specified purposes.

Below:
Decisions on the future of unremunerative passenger services should be made by the Minister, said the Select Committee. Stanier 2-6-4T No 42600 stands at Leek with a local train for Uttoxeter.
G. S. Robinson

Left:
Crew training for the Manchester-Crewe electric services continued throughout the summer. New 'AM4' class electric multiple-unit No 009 was photographed at Wilmslow on 21 July 1960.
Alan H. Bryant

- British Railways' accounts should reflect only the matters under their control, so that both the BTC and the Minister would be clearly accountable to Parliament for their separate responsibilities.

Of all the schemes then in progress, it was the London Midland's main line electrification which came closest to cancellation. The projected costs of £118 million had risen alarmingly to £161 million; when the first section opened from Crewe to Manchester Piccadilly on 12 September (Crewe-Liverpool followed on 1 January 1962), there was considerable doubt as to whether the catenary would be extended south of Crewe. In *The Guardian's* view, this would 'have been a wretched end to an ambitious project'. Fortunately, the Minister, Ernest Marples, subsequently allowed the work to continue, but that was the end of major electrification schemes for many years.

In fairness, the Government should also have shouldered a part of the blame for the failures. But, in the end, something had to go, and the Commission was abolished for operational purposes at the close of 1962.

Below:
Permanent way mechanisation was still in its infancy in 1960. Here, spent ballast is being loaded into wagons for removal on the St Margarets loop in East Grinstead. *G. S. Robinson*

Glasgow Debacle

There can have been few things more calculated to increase public scepticism of railway modernisation than the spectacular technical failure which overtook the Glasgow 'Blue Trains' in December 1960.

The ailing suburban services in the Glasgow area were, by common consent, prime candidates for electrification, and work was put in hand with alacrity. The initial lines to be treated were the Helensburgh Central/Balloch/Milngavie-Queen Street-Springburn/Airdrie/Bridgeton Central services, which were formally opened by the Chairman of the BTC Sir Brian Robertson on 5 November 1960. On that day, apart from the peak services and a skeleton timetable during the afternoon and early evening, booked services were cancelled to enable steam locomotives and coaching stock to be removed from the area and to permit the cleaning up of the tunnel sections, and the assembly of the new electric multiple-units at their berthing points ready for the commencement of the full services. The highly regarded trains built by Pressed Steel with AEI electrical equipment had already successfully completed several thousand miles of trials.

Sunday 6 November was spent in a (second) full-scale dress rehearsal of the new weekday timetable; the public were invited to take part, and 15,000 did so. Normal service commenced the following day. Much effort went into planning the publicity and integrated colour schemes which sought to associate yellow with westbound trains and blue with eastbound. Fast, comprehensive and frequent services were provided, combining to offer eight trains hourly through Queen Street Low Level in each direction.

The initial target of doubling traffic was quickly achieved, with over 400,000 carried in the first week compared with 170,000 in 1959. But, following earlier minor incidents, as the 07.00 Balloch-Bridgeton was nearing Renton in thick fog on 13 December, a transformer explosion occurred. This ripped open the roof and a bulkhead, and eight people needed hospital

Right:
Glasgow suburban services were obvious candidates for conversion to electric traction due to the heavy loads carried. Before the arrival of the 'Blue Trains', ex-LNER Class V3 2-6-2T No 67627 approaches Coatbridge (Sunnyside) with the 1.01pm Anniesland-Airdrie on 17 August 1959. *B. Aylard*

treatment. Another but less damaging failure happened the next day. Two further mishaps took place on 17 December, and at 01.38 on Sunday 18 December and 17 units unserviceable, the decision was made to withdraw the electric trains and restore the steam service. Coaching stock and locomotives were hurriedly recalled, new timetables and rosters compiled, electric sets were stored, and supplies of coal and water etc found. To the everlasting credit of those concerned, a steam service was operated against all the odds on the Monday morning.

The primary trouble was traced to backfiring in the mercury arc rectifiers, and the transformers had to be rebuilt; the cause of the backfiring was put down to overheating or excessive temperature differentials. As a result of the Glasgow troubles and other failures on the northeast London electrics, many recommendations were made by the Inspecting Officer of Railways, particularly with regard to equipment simplification and reliability. Elimination of the 6.25/25kV changeover was seen as a substantial contribution to reliability, and tests were made to see if clearances could be safely reduced. As a result, the whole of the London Midland electrification was completed at 25kV ac.

Electric traction in Glasgow was restored on 1 October 1961.

Above:
Two 'Blue Trains' stand in the sidings at Airdrie alongside the station. *S. Rickard*

Left:
A three-car Pressed Steel set pauses at Dalmuir Park with the 2.30pm Bridgeton-Balloch. In later years, flat glass was substituted for the rounded windscreens on these units as an anti-vandal measure.
S. Rickard

1960

Right:
Fish traffic left the railway for good later in the decade, but in 1960 a new MacFisheries depot was opened at Finsbury Park. On the night of 27 August boxes of fish are being transferred from the blue spot fish vans to waiting road trailers. *Ian Allan Library*

Below:
Although displaced from the principal Great Eastern services by the new Type 4 diesels, the 'Britannia' Pacifics continued to show their capabilities on other services. Standard Class 7MT No 70009 *Alfred the Great* arrives at Ipswich with an up Yarmouth express via Beccles on 5 March 1960. *John C. Baker*

Above:
The Western Region advertised the Swansea & District Holiday Express for those who could stand five consecutive days out by train!

Top left:
The 'Chenford' electrification was inaugurated on 21 November. A trial train of the new stock intended for the Chingford and Enfield branches led by unit No 417 with GEC equipment stands at Rye House on 2 June. *BR*

Above left:
Station reconstruction was part of the package at Broxbourne and, as seen here, at Harlow Town, opened on 13 July. The appointments were lavish, but even so passengers had to negotiate two staircases to reach any platform from the entrance. *BR*

Left:
A massive embankment landslide at Hook on 27 December left only two tracks usable on the South Western main line. Emergency crossovers were installed, and Class N15 4-6-0 No 30765 *Sir Gareth* was photographed hauling an up train slowly over the down fast line. *G. S. Robinson*

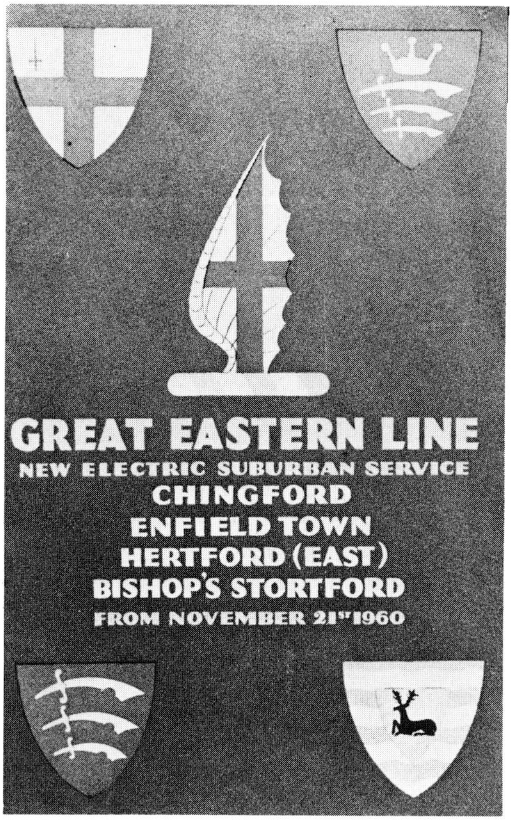

Right:
Cover of the timetable booklet containing the new electric services.

Far right:
To stimulate interest amongst the local youth, Great Eastern management organised a Progress Chaser's competition for which special low fares were available. Plaques were to be presented to schools as well as the prizes for the individuals.

Below:
The Bluebell Railway reopened (for the second time) in 1960, but only between Sheffield Park and a point short of Horsted Keynes. Ex-SECR 'P' class 0-6-0T No 323 *Bluebell* stands at the terminus with the former London Transport Chesham coaches on 8 July 1961.
John Glover

1961

'The year 1961 was not a good year financially for the Commission's undertaking as a whole, the result being a deficit of £122 million compared with a deficit of £101 million in 1960. As has been usual in recent years, however, this overall result was dominated by the large losses of British Railways' — BTC Annual Report.

Right:
BR Standard Class 4MT 2-6-0 No 76034 arrives at Yarmouth Vauxhall with empty stock for a summer Saturday departure for the Midlands in May. Three years previously this train would have run via the M&GN route. The extreme age of so much of the coaching stock is only too apparent.
John C. Baker

A New Chairman

Sir Brian Robertson retired from the Chairmanship of the British Transport Commission on 31 May 1961, a post which he had held since 1953. His services were recognised by the conferment of a peerage in the Birthday Honours list.

Dr Richard Beeching, former Technical Director of ICI, took over the next day. Appointed at the then unheard-of salary of £24,000 per annum, the first press conference held within a few days demonstrated his grip. Already he was clear that modernisation alone would not lead to viability; immediate drastic curtailment of the programme would be a mistake, but some modification would be necessary in the later stages. Too optimistic a view had been taken of the financial benefits, particularly in the earlier stages when benefits from partial modernisation would be small and disturbance great. This applied particularly to the London Midland electrification. On the other hand, earlier stages of modernisation were beginning to yield substantial improvements in operating efficiency, and there was a general improvement in punctuality.

Dr Beeching stressed that it was his intention to root out the basic causes of the declining financial situation rather than attempt cosmetic changes. So once again a series of studies was to be undertaken, and it was promised that these would be more comprehensive and far-reaching than anything done in the past. They were directed towards the following ends:

- Determination in detail of the costs of handling existing traffics by existing methods.
- Determination of the forms of traffic which railways do handle, or could handle, more satisfactorily than other forms of transport.
- Determination of the volumes of traffic flowing through all stations and depots, and over all route miles of the railway system, to establish the present level of occupation of capacity, the revenue-earning ability and the profitability of particular parts of the system or particular services.

Below:
Coal traffic was self-supporting. Class WD 2-8-0 No 90185 comes off the East Lincolnshire line at Spalding Town with an up coal train in July 1961. *John C. Baker*

Left:
Local railways would be suspect wherever they operated. The Dunton Green-Westerham branch was one such, and closed completely on 30 October 1961. It was photographed shortly before closure at the Westerham terminus, with ex-SECR 'H' class 0-4-0T No 31263 on the push-pull set. *G. S. Robinson*

- Determination of the pattern of traffic flows throughout the country both by rail and other modes, to establish what volume of traffic favourable to rail is available and how it moves.
- Determination of how the railway system of freight carrying can best be modified to attract the maximum amount of remunerative traffic.

Everything was thus still to be decided. But already it was clear to the listeners that the results might well be uncomfortable. Dr Beeching was even then convinced that there was too little traffic trying to justify too much cost, and that there was an awful lot of the system which represented a drain on its resources while contributing little to its wellbeing. By the end of 1961 views had hardened; long-distance passenger traffic, coal and minerals and commuter traffic in London (and perhaps elsewhere) were either self-supporting or potentially so. General merchandise would have a future with new methods of handling. 'A system shaped to provide these services, *but freed from unsuitable traffics* (Author's italics), promises to be viable.' Thus the 1961 Annual Report.

Below:
New 'Western' class Type 4 No D1007 *Western Talisman* passes Saltney Junction, Chester, with a Paddington-Birkenhead express. How justified was the maintenance of a four-track main line, especially when an express might run to six coaches only? *Derek Cross*

The Wisdom of Dieselisation

In many ways, modernisation had been a miserably frustrating experience for British Railways, which had resulted in much deserved public sympathy. But the shiny new equipment seemed to produce little public benefit, and by the time the 1,000th main line diesel was delivered questions were increasingly being asked. Where indeed were all the improved services which had been promised and paid for?

Some of the answer lay in the difficulties associated with partial implementation of the dieselisation programme. Train timings had to make allowances for mixed steam/diesel operation, and locomotive rosters could not immediately exploit the capabilities of the new machines. Then the failures started, an area which it had been said that the new diesels would score over steam. Given the way in which series production had suddenly overtaken the pilot scheme, some trouble was not altogether surprising, but cut little ice with the public. A particular problem was the train-heating boilers, which caused over one-quarter of all locomotive casualties; cold trains in winter added to the discontent. And in many locomotive classes, service experience brought out further faults, some with serious and expensive consequences.

It also seemed that other departments of the railway had not fully appreciated what the diesels meant for the business. Whilst the locomotives had the capability of increased utilisation, where was the training to ensure that the operators exploited it? The Civil Engineer, fearful of the effects of the small wheels on the tracks, had already imposed such restrictive conditions that not only were the locomotives underpowered for the work they were intended to do, but they were given additional axles purely for load-bearing purposes and which unnecessarily increased their weight.

Below:
The Midland was forever willing to use two small engines when one big one would have done. A pair of the short-lived Metrovick Type 2 diesels, Nos D5712/3 approach Mill Hill Broadway with an afternoon St Pancras-Derby-Manchester Central service. Use of two engines did at least minimise the disruption should one fail. *John Glover*

Below right:
New locomotive deliveries continued. BTH 800hp Type 1 No D8228 pauses at Bury St Edmunds en route from acceptance trials at Doncaster to Ipswich. *John C. Baker*

Left:
Standard Class 2MT 2-6-0 No 78049 arrives at Coldstream with a local from Berwick to St Boswells in August 1961, and leaves behind a smoky haze. It is easy to forget just how dirty the railways were when operated by steam traction.
John C. Baker

Maintenance arrangements also tended to be less well thought out than they might have been; adequate facilities and staff preparation were essential for this relatively complex machinery compared with steam. The LMR were particularly low on specialised maintenance depots and this was reflected in their diesel fleet, with mileages as low as 230 per day for the BR/Sulzer Type 4s being alleged.

Goodwill for the railway ebbed away, and calls were heard for, if not a return to steam, at least a halt to the diesel programme. But steam's disadvantages were growing ever more obvious; the crux of these was perhaps the dirt and filth, not just for the labour problem of getting train crews and maintenance staff, but in addition the growing public concern for the environment as expressed then through the 'smokeless zone' legislation. Such considerations were valid, irrespective of any power output or efficiency improvements which have been possible with further development of the steam locomotive. The publication of comparative cost figures was reassuring, if only slightly! These showed that the diesels were giving increasing economies at the higher mileages, a conclusion deemed as highly satisfactory.

Comparative Costs

	Steam Class 7MT			*Type 4 Diesel 2,300hp*		
Miles per day	100	200	480	100	200	480
All costs in (new) pence per mile at contemporary (1960) prices						
Interest and renewals	5.2	2.7	1.0	19.7	9.8	4.2
Operating costs:						
Stabling and servicing	7.9	4.2	2.1	3.7	1.9	0.8
Fuel, water and lubricants	16.3	16.3	16.3	7.9	7.9	7.9
Maintenance	12.7	10.4	8.1	10.4	8.3	6.7
Train crews	6.2	6.2	6.2	5.8	5.8	5.8
Totals	48.3	39.8	33.7	47.5	33.7	25.4

The Riding of Coaches

The design and development of railway rolling stock over the years owed much to empirical methods, and little to theory and research. The British Railways standard coach which first appeared in 1950 was the result of an urgent requirement to replace company-designed vehicles, many of which were antique in all respects, and to compensate for the lack of new construction during the war years. The continued existence of large quantities of what later became known as Mk 1 vehicles is eloquent testimony to the excellence of the basic design and construction.

One of the unsatisfactory aspects was the riding qualities. The Mk 1 coaches were originally fitted with a bogie design based on a GWR pattern. Although very acceptable when new or recently repaired, performance quickly deteriorated as wear accumulated in the axlebox guides and the spring suspension gear, and trouble was arising at mileages as low as 40,000. 'Hunting', or violent oscillation of the bogie at speeds, was a particularly unpleasant sensation, and tended to be more pronounced on long-welded rails. The increase in vehicle utilisation and the general raising of speeds under modernisation meant that a nuisance quickly and justifiably became a source of major public complaint.

The suspension of rail vehicles has proved to be one of the more intractable engineering tasks facing designers of rolling stock, since the ideal suspension system has to satisfy a number of objectives. These range from keeping the wheels in contact with the rail under all conditions of curvature and cant, to the limiting of the transmission of shocks to the body which may arise from sources as diverse as rail joints and brake applications. What is more, the result must be constant irrespective of the load in the

Below:
The Metro-Schlieren bogie was tried beneath a trio of second class compartment vehicles of Mk 1 type, and is seen here fitted to M25282, a Metro-Cammell-built coach of 1958. *BR*

Above:
The B4 bogie built at Swindon turned out to be the answer to the British Transport Commission's prayer. *BR*

vehicle. At the same time, maintenance costs must be contained. Such was the urgency of the problem, that solutions were pursued on three fronts:

- Long-term theoretical work, which involved the development of a new high-speed bogie for future adoption.
- Investigation to see what could be achieved at modest cost through minor rebuilds, different maintenance procedures and improvements such as the fitting of roller bearings.
- Substitution of other bogie designs. In the late 1950s, trials were run with bogies from Andre Neidhart and Metalastik, both making much use of rubber, and Schlieren, a successful continental design.

Even the above programmes could not adequately meet the need in the time scale demanded, and the well-tried Gresley bogies were fitted retrospectively to many catering vehicles. A more promising development was the Commonwealth bogie of American origin, which relied upon a compensation arrangement which transferred weight between axles. The result was truly excellent, and they became a standard fitting in 1960.

The Commonwealth bogie gains had their costs in increased weight (6½ tons) and complex adjustment methods. They were also found unsuitable for use unmodified on third rail electrified lines. So the emergence of the Swindon-designed B4 bogie was greeted with relief. For a start it was nearly 1½ tons lighter than the Commonwealth, which was the equivalent of an extra coach in a 10-coach train. It also had a cheaper price tag, and proved economical on maintenance. Full-scale trials of 50 bogies were carried out on the Western Region in 1961, and the design was fitted to all locomotive-hauled coaching stock built from 1963 onwards.

The research effort then turned to the wagon fleet, which had become prone to a distressing habit of jumping off the rails at speeds above 45mph.

The 'Deltics'

One of the shortcomings of the initial dieselisation plans was the lack of any orders for locomotives with much more than 2,000hp. To some extent, this reflected the lack of any commercial engine then on the market which could produce anything like 3,000hp given size and axle-loading constraints. There *was* a way of doing this using a pair of the 1,650hp Napier Deltics, which were intricate but compact 18-cylinder opposed piston designs developed for use in small naval craft. They were highly unconventional, but English Electric had successfully used them in their demonstration locomotive in 1955.

But what market would there be for such a powerful locomotive? The *Deltic* prototype had certainly showed its remarkable capability in service and on test, but as the main lines were to be electrified it was thought to have little application. Circumstances changed when the East Coast main line electrification was abandoned, and the Eastern Region became convinced that this locomotive alone offered the performance it was looking for, wanting it despite a supposedly outrageous price. Eventually the Region got its way, and deliveries started in 1961.

Once some initial teething troubles had been overcome, the 'Deltics' were set to work with a vengeance. To ensure that these complex machines attained their planned availability for traffic, a unique maintenance agreement was concluded under which the work was carried out by the manufacturer. The agreement was geared to the performance of the locomotives, and if this fell below a specified mileage, a penalty clause in the contract reduced the sum BR had to pay. The contract was initially for five years, and subsequently renewed.

The 22 'Deltics' replaced 55 steam locomotives on express passenger duties between King's Cross, Leeds, Newcastle and Scotland, and the standards of performance set exceeded anything that had then been seen in Britain. The 1962 summer timetable showed 15 trains from London to Newcastle, 268.4 miles, with an average time of 4hr 59min — a frequency of express service without parallel in Europe over so great a distance. Gradual improvement continued for many years, as civil engineering restrictions were eased and the 'Deltic's' 100mph capability was fully exploited.

Below:
Another Finsbury Park locomotive, No D9018 *Ballymoss* approaches York with the 12.00 King's Cross-Newcastle on 27 May 1962. Note the 1957 Cravens prototype coach, third from the locomotive. *P. J. Lynch*

Left:
The Institution of Locomotive Engineers celebrated their Golden Jubilee in May and a special exhibition of locomotives and rolling stock was staged in Marylebone Goods Yard. Newly delivered and still unnamed 'Deltic' Type 5 diesel No D9003 was one of the exhibits.
John Glover

The appearance was impressive, especially in the original livery of Brunswick green with a lime green 'skirt', offset by off-white window surrounds and a grey roof. The buffer beam was red, and all running gear black. The noise was thunderous, and the exhaust fumes choking. The allocations were eight each to Haymarket and Finsbury Park, and seven to Gateshead, and remained thus until the locomotives were displaced from the top link jobs. Originally, all were to be named after racehorses in the best LNER tradition, but the authorities in the North and Scotland opted instead for no doubt worthy but boring regimental names. As built they weighed a fraction under 100 tons (an improvement on the prototype), with a splendid 33hp/ton rating; by comparison the BR/Sulzer Type 4 could manage only 18hp/ton.

If there is any cause for regret over the 'Deltic' saga, it must be just a little sadness that the fleet was never expanded.

The 'Deltic' Names and Allocations when new

D9000	*Royal Scots Grey*	Haymarket
D9001	*St Paddy*	Finsbury Park
D9002	*The King's Own Yorkshire Light Infantry*	Gateshead
D9003	*Meld*	Finsbury Park
D9004	*Queen's Own Highlander*	Haymarket
D9005	*The Prince of Wales Own Regiment of Yorkshire*	Gateshead
D9006	*The Fife and Forfar Yeomanry*	Haymarket
D9007	*Pinza*	Finsbury Park
D9008	*The Green Howards*	Gateshead
D9009	*Alycidon*	Finsbury Park
D9010	*The King's Own Scottish Borderer*	Haymarket
D9011	*The Royal Northumberland Fusiliers*	Gateshead
D9012	*Crepello*	Finsbury Park
D9013	*The Black Watch*	Haymarket
D9014	*The Duke of Wellington's Regiment*	Gateshead
D9015	*Tulyar*	Finsbury Park
D9016	*Gordon Highlander*	Haymarket
D9017	*The Durham Light Infantry*	Gateshead
D9018	*Ballymoss*	Finsbury Park
D9019	*Royal Highland Fusilier*	Haymarket
D9020	*Nimbus*	Finsbury Park
D9021	*Argyll and Sutherland Highlander*	Haymarket

1961

Right:
A last look at the old Euston before wholesale demolition took place. Stanier 4MT 2-6-4T No 42611 is ready to take empty stock out of No 2 platform on the former arrival side to the carriage sidings. *John Glover*

Below:
The Marylebone exhibition provided an opportunity for the public to see modern motive power from all over the country. GT3, the privately sponsored gas turbine built on a steam locomotive chassis, stood next to No E3057, one of the Doncaster-built ac electric locomotives of Class AL5 on 15 May 1961. *John Glover*

Above:
The pioneer electrified line using ac for traction was that between Lancaster, Morecambe and Heysham. It was converted to ac in 1953, using old ex-LMSR stock. The 1.55pm Lancaster Castle-Morecambe Promenade restarts from Scale Hall on 28 October 1961. The line closed completely on the first day of 1966. *Noel A. Machell*

Above left:
Only the Peppercorn 'A1' Pacifics of the LNER among the express classes failed to find a candidate for preservation. On 28 August 1961, No 60158 *Aberdonian* coasts through Oakleigh Park in the north London suburbs with a Hull-King's Cross train.
John Glover

Left:
Quite the shiniest object in Halifax, to judge from this view of 14 September 1961, is the BRCW-built Calder Valley DMU. The new unit is forming a Bradford Exchange-Huddersfield train, seen here entering the station.
P. J. Lynch

Above:
No less than 15 diesel shunter types of under 350hp were produced in the 1950s, some in penny numbers only. Few of the non-standard designs lasted beyond 1970. The styling of these machines was rarely a strong point; the 204hp Andrew Barclay 0-6-0DMs of 1956 had the fuel tank in front of the driver's cab! No 11183 (later D2406) shunts at Kings Lynn in April 1961. *John C. Baker*

Right:
The 1960s coincided with a peak interest in train spotting, and the Ian Allan spotters' books were to be found everywhere. At the height of the steam/diesel changeover, six books were being issued every six months, though as the steam stock dwindled, the numbers reduced again. There were also specialist books, such as one on headcodes and another on London Transport Railways. A selection of the covers of the period is shown. *John Glover*

1962

'This year 1962 is witnessing the greatest advance in the speed, frequency and systematisation of passenger train services ever known in Great Britain within the limits of a single 12-month period' — *Trains Illustrated* editorial.

Right:
The Pullman Car Co ceased to be a separate entity at the end of 1962, and became a wholly owned subsidiary of the British Railways Board under the BT Hotels organisation. All three of the 5-BEL 'Brighton Belle' units can be seen in this picture of the last down evening service from Victoria on 24 July 1962. Unit No 3052 is passing the Pullman works at Preston Park.
Ian Allan Library

Commercial Freedom

The 1962 Transport Act was intended to give the railways a new start. The British Railways Board opened their doors for business on 1 January 1963, with much wider commercial discretion than the railways had enjoyed hitherto. Gone were the last vestiges of the days of the common carrier, where anything and everything had to be accepted in the way of goods for conveyance, at reasonable charges and for which the carrier had what amounted to a total liability for their safe transit.

The Board were given the freedom to accept traffic at whatever rates they chose to charge. This applied to passengers and goods alike, save only when some monopoly powers were thought to exist. Thus, in the London area passenger fares proposals had to be submitted to the Transport Tribunal for scrutiny and the hearing of objections before they could be implemented. Coastal shipping was also protected against uneconomic rate cutting by the railways. Whilst London fares, including those of London Transport, continued to excite public interest from time to time, the coastal shipping provision was invoked once only, in 1964. Complaints were made about rail charges for china clay traffic between Fowey and Sittingbourne; British Railways were ordered

Below:
Even the smallest stations had their own cartage facility. On the Far North line at Helmsdale, a rigid four-wheel lorry is on hand, and the postman meets the train.
G. S. Robinson

to raise their charges, but retained the traffic!

The Act relieved the Board of any social duty to continue services. Whatever railway management may have thought about the effects on communities of closing unremunerative lines, this became solely a matter for the Minister, who could judge his response based upon a report on the hardship which would ensue and submitted by the local Transport Users' Consultative Committee. Despite the Select Committee's recommendations, there was no provision for the Minister to grant-aid the Board for any closures which he refused.

Other features were the ability to develop surplus land and to construct and be an operator of pipelines. Manufacturing for outside concerns remained a prohibited area, and the workshops were thus able to seek orders only from the nationalised transport sector.

Yet, for all the apparent opportunity offered, the Board were slow to take advantage. Perhaps notions of equity and public service die hard, but it was not until 1968 and after being pushed by the Prices and Incomes Board that the pricing of passenger fares according to the market was introduced. Once started, there was no stopping what became known as selective pricing, but the failure to reap greater profits by charging much higher fares on routes where high quality services were offered was seen by some as a major shortcoming of the Beeching years.

Below:
In a timetable mention of freight train facilities in 1962, it was stated that 'The Railways undertake the transfer of complete farms, including implements, livestock, etc, from one part of the country to another. Special arrangements can be made to enable cows to travel between milking times, or, where very long journeys are involved, for them to be milked en route, and all animals to be fed and watered.' Time has indeed passed on since then.

Left:
In the London area so called, the Transport Tribunal was given the task of keeping an avuncular eye upon charging arrangements. At Grange Road, which just qualified to be included, a dog and a pram have each been carried at half the adult fare. These charging rates were, however, levied nationally. *G. S. Robinson*

Kent Coast Electrification Complete

The South-Eastern Division of the Southern was given priority in modernisation due to the tremendous growth of population in Kent, and the fact that electrification had been halted, partially complete, by the war. Of the two main lines, that serving the Medway towns was the obvious choice for the initial work. Phase 1 extended the third rail from Gillingham to Faversham, then Ramsgate and Dover, plus the Sheerness branch in June 1959. Work on Phase 2 began immediately afterwards, and this electrified from Sevenoaks via Tonbridge to Ashford and on to Ramsgate both via Folkestone and Canterbury West, including also Paddock Wood-Maidstone West and Maidstone East-Ashford, and also the Folkestone Harbour branch. Electric trains were able to begin operating in steam timings during 1961, but the full electric timetable had to await the completion of resignalling and other engineering work in June 1962.

An ambitious timetable was operated from 18 June, and featured much dividing and combining of trains in traditional Southern manner:

Phase 1

- 0.40: Victoria to Ramsgate, with a portion detached at Gillingham for Dover Priory.
- 0.14: Victoria to Gillingham and Maidstone East, extended to Sheerness and Ashford (in Phase 2) respectively.
- 0.36: Dover to Sheerness and return.
- Shuttle service: Sittingbourne to Sheerness.
- 0.40: Charing Cross to Gillingham semi-fast via Woolwich, extended to Ramsgate as stopping service.

Phase 2

- 0.00: Charing Cross fast to Ashford, then Folkestone and all stations to Ramsgate; portion detached at Ashford running via Canterbury West to Ramsgate.
- 0.10: Charing Cross semi-fast to Tonbridge, dividing with front for Paddock Wood, Ashford, then all stations to Margate via Folkestone, and rear all stations to Ashford.
- 0.49: Victoria to Margate; semi-fast to Ashford, then all stations via Canterbury West.
- Boat trains: Six daily services, with 16 down and 32 up conditional paths.

The improvements were substantial, almost doubling the number of services and reducing journey times by about one-third. To operate the services, new multiple-unit rolling stock was constructed. 112 4-car express (4-CEP/4-BEP) units were allocated, together with 182 2-car semi-fast (2-HAP) units and 10

Motor Luggage Vans for use on the non-electrified quaysides. For servicing and maintenance, a central repair depot was constructed at Chart Leacon, Ashford, and equipped to deal with heavy repairs; the Ramsgate carriage sheds were also extended and carried out light repairs. Freight and parcels traffic, and also the prestige 'Golden Arrow' and 'Night Ferry' services were hauled either by the Doncaster-built No E5000 series electric locomotives, or by the BRCW Type 3 diesels.

Extensive engineering work included the quadrupling in the London area to Swanley, between Rainham and Newington, and from Cheriton to Folkestone. Part of the Sheerness branch was doubled, and capacity generally enhanced. Resignalling provided for 2½min headways on the main line to Ramsgate with Phase 1, and 3min to Dover with Phase 2. Platforms were extended at over 60 stations.

Kent was lucky to have the provision of such lavish facilities well on the way to completion before the spending constraints were imposed.

Above:
Before the Kent Coast electrification was inaugurated, the last steam-hauled 'Golden Arrow' passes Paddock Wood behind 'West Country' Pacific No 34100 *Appledore*. On the left, a rail-tour to Hawkhurst awaits the last of the '01' class No 31065. The date is 11 June 1961. *P. J. Lynch*

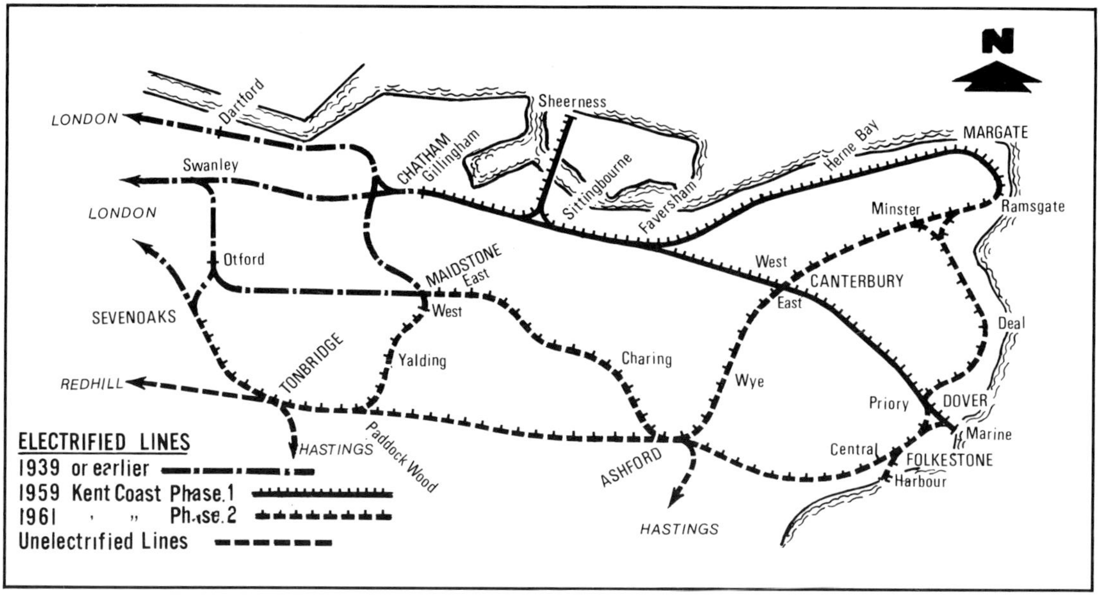

The Railway Workshops

It was 1962 before the railway workshop issue was tackled, but the speed and manner with which the proposals were announced precipitated a one-day strike on 3 October. For once, press and public had much sympathy with the railwaymen, and the consensus was that the issue was badly mishandled by the BTC and Government alike.

The case for rationalisation was irrefutable. The main works, totalling 29, were then employing 60,000 men, with spare capacity already at a quarter and rising fast. Re-equipment of the railways had meant substantial orders going to the private sector, especially for locomotives, ever since railway management decided not to embark on design or manufacture of diesel engines, transmissions or electric traction equipment. Nor was it only new building; the improved productivity of a diesel fleet compared with steam required fewer locomotives, each of which needed less maintenance. Thus although all repair work had been kept as a railway workshops activity, the volume was falling at an accelerating pace.

A glance at the Appendices to this volume will show just how fast this process was happening. With wagons and with coaches, the aim was to pare the rolling stock down to a level that would find regular employment throughout the year, and tighter systems of control would reduce the numbers still further. At that date, the average wagon made a loaded trip only once in an incredible 12 days; the scope for improvement was evident.

Before 1962, each of the Regions retained control of its workshops, with the result that construction and repair work of all description was scattered around the country reflecting the pre-1948 (and perhaps even the pre-1923) needs. The setting up of a Workshops Division was thus a prerequisite to reorganisation. There was then a bald announcement in September: 12 of the 29 workshops would close within three years, and the workforce would be cut to 38,000. Whilst there had been some expectation of

Right:
The Stanier '8F' 2-8-0s were built in the workshops of three of the 'Big Four' as well as private manufacturers. Crewe Works sees Brighton-built No 48697 receiving attention.
P. L. Simpson

Left:
Although some of the main line diesel fleet was built in BR Workshops like this Derby-built Bo-Bo Type 2, the Sulzer engine and BTH traction motors were bought-in items. The picture shows the prototype being lowered on to its bogies; subsequent batches were built at Crewe and Darlington, as well as by Beyer Peacock. *BR*

such a move by the unions, and perhaps even an element of resigned acceptance, the total lack of consultation or any indication that the social aspects were considered at all caused consternation and the result already recorded. And if with hindsight this seems a muted response, it should be remembered that this was the first time a national rail strike had taken place since the General Strike in 1926.

The works listed for closure were: Bromsgrove, Caerphilly, Cowlairs, Darlington (Loco), Darlington (Faverdale), Earlestown, Gorton, Lancing, Stratford (Loco), Stratford (Carriage), Walker Gate and Wolverhampton. The closure of Ashford Works had already been announced.

There is no doubt that the BTC had ample justification for the action they took, and perhaps should have taken rather earlier than was the case. Fortunately, it also appears that in the event few employees suffered much hardship. However, as an exercise in industrial relations it was a disaster, and left the nation wondering what next would emerge from the Beeching regime.

Left:
Inside Swindon Works 'A' shop, an unidentified 'Castle' class 4-6-0 was photographed alongside 'Hall' 4-6-0 No 6905 *Claughton Hall* in July 1962.
J. W. Rainey

Boundary Changes

At the time of nationalisation, arguments had ranged back and forth about the positioning of Regional boundaries; should Scotland be separate, and was a basis of 'lines' bringing, for instance, the London Midland Region to Bristol via the former LMS route preferable to geographical territories? Certainly, the original Regions differed greatly in size, from the LMR with 4,993 route miles down to the North Eastern with only 1,823. In 1962, a further review took place, and sweeping changes were introduced on 1 January 1963.

The intention was the elimination of dual administration at Birmingham and Exeter, by then the only two centres where this existed. 'Consideration of the volume, nature, areas of origin and directions of flow of existing traffic, and of the future traffic potential, caused the Birmingham area . . . to be placed wholly under the control of the LMR.' In reality, the writing was already on the wall for the Western Region's line to Wolverhampton and Birkenhead; with electrification from Euston due within a few years, many of the WR services were to sink into eventual oblivion. This in turn paved the way to the closure of Birmingham Snow Hill leaving New Street, then in the throes of rebuilding, and Moor Street to cater for the remaining passenger traffic via new spurs at Bordesley and Smethwick. Freightwise, the new Bescot yard was accessible from all directions without touching the New Street station area. Lines west and north of Shrewsbury were also gained by the LMR.

Further south, the Southern Region ceded all of its territory west of Salisbury to Paddington. The BTC felt that the lines were so intermingled (with the famous arrangement that WR and SR trains leaving Exeter St Davids in the northerly direction on parallel tracks would be heading for Paddington and Plymouth respectively), that unified control was the only sensible solution. It would at least have ended the most conspicuous anachronism, that of separate diesel multiple-unit schemes for the WR South Devon and SR East Devon services, based as they were on their 'own' stations at Exeter and with precious little to connect them. In the

Right:
The '0298' class Beattie 2-4-0WT locomotives on the Wenfordbridge line did not wait to see Western Region ownership as they were displaced during the summer by three WR 0-6-0PTs. No 30587 simmers as it awaits its next turn of duty.
G. S. Robinson

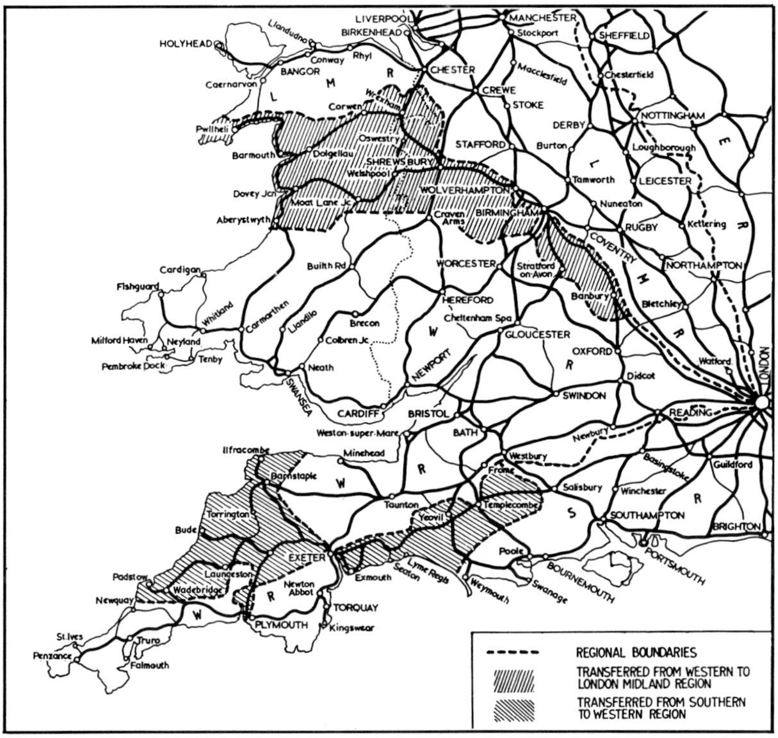

event, the deferred SR scheme was left so long that the branches nearly closed first, with the exception of Exmouth which remained open. In North Devon, only the Ilfracombe line as far as Barnstaple has survived, with the freight branch to Meldon Quarry, but the former GWR branches fared little better.

On the main lines, unified control was an obvious prelude to rationalisation, and in 1962 the betting was on the elimination of the WR Westbury main line in view of the paucity of settlement between Newbury and Taunton. This was not to be, partly because of the need for reversal at St Davids for all through trains, had traffic been concentrated on the Waterloo route. The former LSWR main line west of Salisbury became a guinea pig for cost reduction, and long stretches were later singled.

Left:
'2251' class 0-6-0 No 3200 stands below the castle at Harlech on the Cambrian coast, awaiting the single line with through coaches Paddington-Pwllheli on 1 September 1961. This was the most distant part of the Western Region to be inherited by Euston.
John Glover

1962

Right:
1962 saw the effective end of main line steam working into King's Cross. In March of that year, Gresley 'A4' Pacific No 60014 *Silver King* displays its corridor tender as it backs down on to its train.
John Glover

Below right:
The diesel-electric *Lion* prototype No D0260 took to the rails in 1962. It was built by an AEI/BRCW/Sulzer consortium, and the manufacturers whose property it remained hoped to win orders from BR in the Type 4 building programme. In ivory livery with gold lining, *Lion* is seen with the up 'Yorkshire Pullman' passing Beeston Junction, south of Leeds. *Ian Allan Library*

Below:
The Southern broke new ground by giving out a booklet with the title *Want to Run a Railway?* to all its commuters. The gist was that the job was a lot more difficult than it looked, and some of the constraints were explained.

Left:
The Scottish Region returned a number of locomotives to traffic in the 1960s for use on enthusiast specials. At the delightful Killin Junction location, NBR 'Glen' class 4-4-0 No 256 *Glen Douglas* propels empty stock into the station. The first two vehicles are restored to Caledonian Railway livery. Behind, Standard Class 4MT No 80092 is in charge of the branch train to Killin on 18 June 1962. *P. J. Lynch*

Below:
A sad line-up of withdrawn NER locomotives was photographed in Darlington North Road scrapyard on 13 March 1962. *P. J. Lynch*

Right:
Yet another farewell railtour saw Standard Class 3MT 2-6-0 No 77003 and the marginally more powerful 4MT No 76046 at Kirby Stephen en route from Darlington to Tebay and Carlisle. The occasion was the end of passenger services over Stainmore, and the date was 20 January 1962.
P. J. Lynch

Above:
The long-standing 'Pines Express' between Manchester and Bournemouth was diverted away from the Somerset & Dorset line with the beginning of the winter timetable. Thereafter, the S&D became purely a local affair. In the last summer of operation on 28 July, Standard Class 4-6-0s Nos 75023 and 73047 approach Masbury with the southbound train. *P. J. Lynch*

Right:
One of the many signal gantries to be replaced by colour lights under modernisation photographed at Greenock Princes Pier on 21 June 1962. *P. J. Lynch*

1963

'If it were done when 'tis done, then 'twere well it were done quickly' — *Macbeth*, quoted by Dr Beeching at his press conference, 25 March 1963

Right:
Millerhill marshalling yard opened in May. It was designed to handle all freight traffic passing via Edinburgh together with coal traffic from the Lothian coalfields. It relaced six small yards. This view shows the up sorting sidings from the hump, with the control tower on the right. *BR*

The Reshaping of British Railways

So extensive had been the trailers for the Reshaping Report, that its contents might well have been guessed by a well informed individual. But presentation counts for a lot, and 35 pages containing nothing but passenger service, line and station closures provided a ready target for the press. The Report contained far more than passenger closures and their justification, but it is the image of the Beeching axe that has lingered with the public.

The proposals in the Report had one purpose: that of shaping the railway towards future viability, without assuming any major changes in their role or their terms of reference. Dr Beeching was said to have written much of it himself. The arguments were set out with admirable clarity. For example, in relation to route costs:

> 'The total cost of providing the route system amounts to nearly a quarter of the railways' total revenue.'
> 'This is a fixed cost . . . quite high traffic densities are necessary, even on single track route, to cover route cost alone.'
> 'One-half of the total route mileage carries about 4% of the total passenger miles. Similarly, one-half of the mileage carries about 5% of the total freight ton miles.'
> 'One-half of the system earns far less than sufficient to cover the cost of providing route to permit the movement, with no allowance whatever for movement or other costs. By contrast, the other half of the system has earnings which cover its route costs more than six times.'

And, after analysis of station and depot revenue:

> 'There can be no question . . . that the railways would be better off financially if a high proportion of the stations were closed, even if this resulted in a total loss of the traffic passing through them.'

The detail could be faulted; for instance, the relating of route costs to revenue rather than the cost structure is at best curious. Similarly, the unequivocal assertion that route costs were totally fixed is now known to be a false assumption. But it did not really matter, so gross were the problems. The hard fact was that much of the system was totally unproductive, and there was no case — even in Beeching's view a social case — for maintaining it.

The benefits from the plan were supposed to arise as shown in the Table on the right.

'Realisation of the savings,' said the Report, 'depends upon adoption of this plan as a whole. Much, though not necessarily all of the deficit should be eliminated by 1970.'

Below:
The archetypal branch line which saw virtual elimination under the Beeching axe. Ex-GWR '57XX' class 0-6-0PT No 3606 takes water at this single line crossing point.
G. S. Robinson

With such a detailed exposé, the way was open for those who disagreed with the proposals to pick holes in the arguments. Why should Liverpool-Southport close when the Southern Region electrified branches remained all but untouched? Why close Aberdare if Merthyr was to stay? What had Prestatyn done to merit closure, when the stations along the Cambrian Coast remained intact? and so on. The more the detail could be faulted, the more the public felt uneasy. The danger was that public concentration on the closure aspects would completely overshadow the improvements to be extracted from the freight business, which were twice as important financially.

Freight was indeed seen as the salvation: liner trains would capture the merchandise market, domestic coal would be concentrated in a few receiving depots, power station coal would be moved in trainloads, sundries traffic would be forcibly concentrated or discarded, wagon utilisation would be vastly improved. There remained large savings to be had by pushing on with dieselisation.

As for the effects of the Plan, the deficit faltered but did not go away. Hindsight suggests that much of Dr Beeching's prescription was a necessary preliminary to building a modern system, but there was not enough in the way of positive proposals. For instance:

- What were the *real* priorities?
- What more could be made of the main line passenger business?
- What scope was there for improvements in labour productivity?
- Were the railways' financial targets capable of being met at all?

All these questions were deferred for the time being, in some cases for many years.

	Estimated financial savings £m per annum
Passenger service withdrawals	18
Passenger line closures	11-13
Freight closures	5-10
Coaching fleet reduction	2-3
Wagon fleet reduction	10-12
Workshop rationalisation	4
Elimination of steam traction	15-20
Cost savings in coal movements	7-10
Sundries concentration	15-20
Liner train net earnings	10-12
Commercial repricing of freight	5-6
Freight volume growth	10-15
Administrative savings	3-4
Total	£115-147 million

Below:
The Reshaping Report.

Passenger Services Improve

The summer timetable commenced on 17 June, with 22 trains now scheduled for start-to-stop runs at 70mph or over, and around 500 at over 60mph. Pride of place was held by the 'Tees-Tyne Pullman', timed at 75.6mph between Darlington and York. Only 23% of the passenger timetable was now worked by steam traction, the diesel proportion alone having increased by more than 15% since 1962.

The Clacton express multiple-units operated a much improved electric service from Liverpool Street, with journey times reduced by up to 28min. They offered the fastest electric service ever scheduled in Great Britain, with start-to-stop times such as 8½min for the 9.6 miles from Shenfield to Chelmsford, and 11½min for the 13 miles from Witham to Colchester. An hourly service was provided. On summer Saturdays, Clacton and Walton had a quite amazing service, with trains leaving London at 20min intervals from 9.40am until 2.00pm and taking between 85 and 91min according to the number of stops.

London Midland Region developments were disappointing; even on the electrified Crewe-Manchester route it seemed inexplicable that new electric locomotives with 100mph capability should be given 45min, with one stop, for the 30.9 miles. Locomotive changing at Crewe added to all journey times, but the 19min allowed for the businessman's 'Lancastrian', the 7.45am Euston-Manchester, seemed almost beyond belief. On the Midland lines, recently revised and greatly accelerated, no changes of note were apparent. The gradual demise of the Great Central was marked by the closure of a number of intermediate stations.

Below:
In 1963 the 'Thames Clyde Express' was a substantial 11-coach formation. Sulzer Type 4 No D163 arrives with the down train on 20 July at Leeds, where the train will reverse for the second time (first reverse at Nottingham) before taking the Skipton route to Carlisle behind the waiting Type 4 in the centre.
J. S. Whiteley

In Scotland, daytime travel between Inverness and London became more possible with an 11hr 44min timing. For sightseers, the Fort William-Mallaig Observation Car was to make double journeys daily at the height of the season. Observation facilities were also to be had on the Glasgow-Fort William, Glasgow-Oban and Inverness-Kyle of Lochalsh routes.

Western Region South Wales services were recast with the winter timetable, with Paddington-Swansea journey times cut by an average of 40min through the use of the 2,700hp 'Western' class diesels. Exact on the hour departures from Paddington and from Cardiff to London on the half-hour were achieved apart from the Pullmans. InterCity DMUs took over all services between Swansea and West Wales, arranged to connect with all main line expresses instead of the through trains provided hitherto. Only the Fishguard boat trains continued as locomotive-hauled workings throughout. These moves, which provided one of the most extensive set of accelerations seen in one timetable, also saw the virtual end of steam traction in the west. Diesel power also took over the Paddington-Cheltenham services. The 'Cheltenham Spa Express' for the first time offered a Cheltenham-London timing of 2hr 20min, and a Gloucester-London time of 2hr dead.

Above:
The Clacton electrics provided a first-rate service to and from Liverpool Street. An eight-car formation prepares to leave the Essex coastal terminus.
G. S. Robinson

Below:
One of the two former 'Devon Belle' observation cars attached to the rear of a Glasgow-Oban train stands at Connel Ferry.
G. G. M. Robinson

The Roadrailer Episode

If merchandise traffic was to be carried door-to-door but using rail for the trunk haul, some means had to be devised for making the road-rail and rail-road transfer for all premises which were not rail-connected. Much thought was expanded upon this problem in the 1950s. With the cost of double handling being prohibitive, the London Midland Region began to experiment in 1959 with the 'Condor'. This nightly train service conveyed containers between Hendon (London) and Gushetfaulds, Glasgow, and the novel pricing structure included collection, conveyance and delivery, irrespective of the contents of the container. Subsequently, large containers were developed for a 'Speedfreight' service between London and Manchester; these two experiments were to become the forerunners of the Freightliner operation, or 'Liner train' in Beeching parlance.

But others had different ideas. If trailer on flat car methods as favoured in the United States were ruled out by the constricted British loading gauge, why not import another American invention, the Railvan? The idea seemed so simple. Basically, the Roadrailer as it became known here, was an ordinary road trailer fitted with two pairs of rear wheels one for road and the other for rail. All that was needed for changeover from one to another was a supply of compressed air to alter the wheel configuration, and a length of track set into a road surface. For transit by road the trailer was attached to an articulated tractor unit in the normal way; by rail each rested on the rear of the one in front, with the leading vehicle coupled to a purpose-built adaptor wagon. The prototype vehicles built by Pressed Steel had a tare of 5 tons and a payload of 11 tons, which was considered promising.

Below:
The standard BR container of the time was an extraordinarily primitive affair. This is the smaller 'A' variety chained to a Conflat wagon. It could take a 4-ton load, but the internal capacity was only 322cu ft (9m^3). *John Glover*

Below right:
The size of the Speedfreight containers is apparent, their cubic capacity being 2.5 times larger than that of the 'A'. Nevertheless, they could still be carried on the standard Conflat. *BR*

Left:
BR/Sulzer Type 2 No D5093 propels the Roadrailer adapter wagon which formed the connection between the conventional locomotive drawgear and the front of the single axle trailers. *BR*

An experimental train was constructed and despatched for trials. Sadly, the system did not live up to expectations. The time taken to assemble and break up trains turned out to be far longer than anticipated and, like Freightliners, the incompatibility with other rolling stock precluded their use other than on routes which could offer whole trainloads of traffic. Instability in operation was said to have been overcome by a design modification. A commercial service between London, Newcastle and Edinburgh was announced for August 1963, but shortly beforehand a coupling broke and the launch was postponed. Later, the project passed to the British Roadrailer Services company in which British Railways had a part interest, but nothing more ever came of it. The economics may have looked good compared with the 4/5-ton capacity BD type containers then in use which had a tare of 2 tons for the container plus another 7 tons for the container flat wagon. However, subsequent developments in both containers and heavy goods vehicles outclassed Roadrailers and BDs alike.

Below:
A photograph of the rear of a train of Roadrailers. There was no brake van, nor was it possible for one to be attached, so the guard rode in the driver's cab.
David C. Smith

The Oil Contracts

One of the year's major achievements in the freight business was the signing of long-term agreements with six major oil companies for the conveyance of petroleum products. The six were Petrofina (GB), Gulf Oil (GB), Mobil Oil Co, Esso Petroleum, Shell Mex and BP Ltd and Regent Oil Co. Six more companies were signed up in the following year, by which time over 200 block trains carrying 90,000 tons of oil products were running every week. The contracts were aimed primarily at increasing train load conveyance from refinery to distribution installations and inland depots, and to the private sidings of large oil consumers. The agreements provided that each company was bound to send by rail in each year in the life of the contract at least the tonnage it forwarded by rail during the 12 months period prior to the agreement coming into force, plus the same proportional increase as that of the total deliveries of oil products for inland consumption. With the anticipated rate of increase in oil consumption, it was confidently believed that the railways would secure over the succeeding 10 years a minimum of 80 million tons, with a potential increase over and above this figure of 25% to 50%.

But, indeed, if the railways could not win this traffic, what hope was there? Despite UK internal movements of oil traffic increasing

Below:
The Fawley-Bromford Bridge trains were the first regular movements of oil in trainloads. Grossing up to 1,200 tons per train, each of which was conveying perhaps 100,000 gallons, three services ran every 24hr. A special working behind Class 9F 2-10-0 No 92152 gains speed through Bromsgrove at the foot of the Lickey Incline on 5 June 1962. The train is banked in the rear by sister locomotive No 92079 and a pair of Class 94XX 0-6-0PTs.
Anthony A. Vickers

by 150% between 1954 and 1962, BR won so little that its market share was halved, with the result that by 1962 only 12½% of the traffic on offer moved by rail. The future prospects were even bleaker, with at least 1½ million tons of oil threatened to be removed from rail by the construction of a Thames-Mersey pipeline, with more to follow. Pipelines though are not the answer to all distribution problems, and heavy fuel oil and bitumen products which require to be kept at relatively high temperatures during transit if they are to flow freely were patently unsuitable for pipeline transmission. These aspects of the industry resulted in the contracts stipulating that BR carryings must share in future growth, as outlined above.

The oil companies were required to provide their own tank wagon fleets and terminal equipment, with fleet replacement of the elderly four-wheelers of nearly 7,000 in number. For Shell Mex and BP alone, this meant an outlay of over £14 million. The new wagons had to be of at least 20 ton capacity (!), and suitable for fast, brake-fitted block train operation, with replacement to be completed within six years. The road hauliers were not expected to suffer from the BR gains, as they would retain the final haul from distribution centre to consumer; rather it was the carriers by water which were expected to lose out. The signing of the contracts represented a bright spot in the year, even if there were gnawing doubts about the profitability of the exercise for the railway.

Below:
A special tank train leaves Thames Haven for Rugby headed by a pair of Brush Type 2 A1A-A1A locomotives. The high capacity tank wagon had yet to be produced. *BR*

Bottom:
A new Brush Type 4 locomotive at the head of a 22-wagon train for Total containing naphtha from Immingham storage depot (seen here) to the North Eastern Gas Board at Leeds. This movement formed part of a 10-year contract.
Ian Allan Library

1963

Above:
The Beeching Report saw little future in the suburban services outside the London area. Electric trains on South Tyneside were withdrawn and replaced by diesel units on 6 January. On Christmas Eve 1962 a four-coach formation of the Eastleigh-built units leaves Pelaw for South Shields. In 1967, de-electrification was applied to the North Tyneside lines also. *I. S. Carr*

Right:
A contemporary advertisement from Metro-Cammell, one of the main private builders of railway rolling stock.

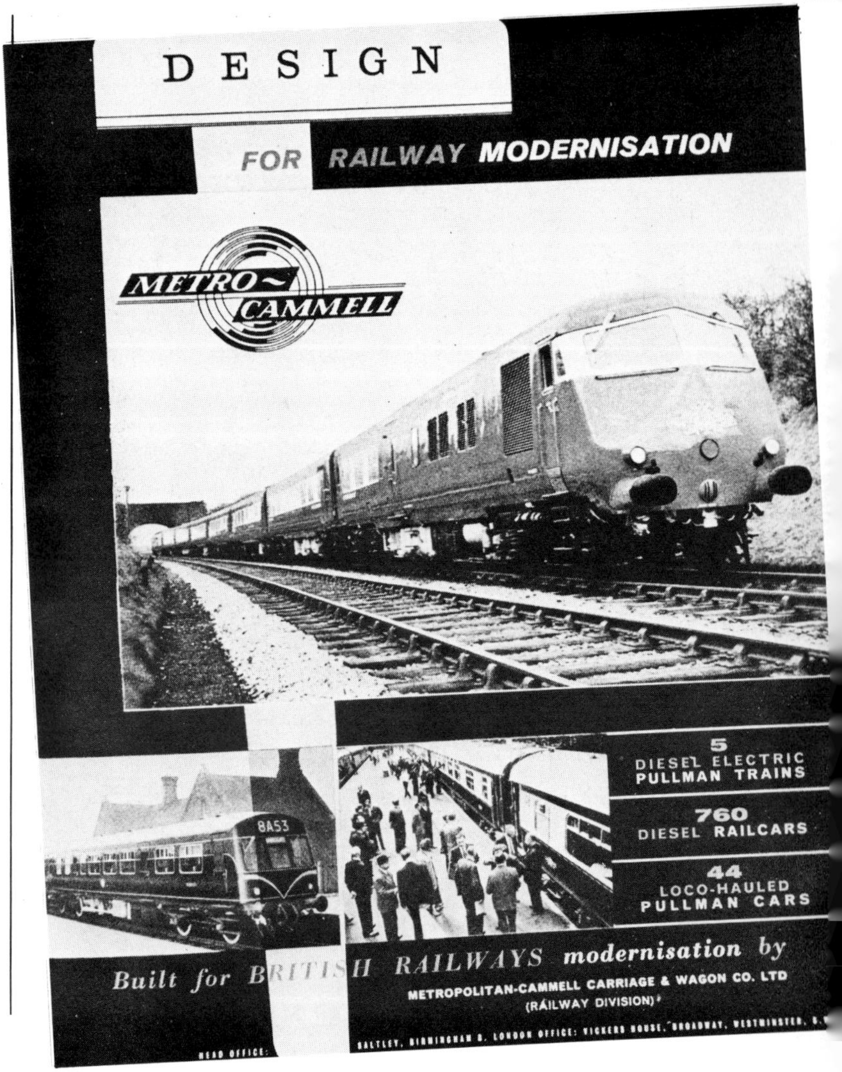

Above:
Closure of all services to Stranraer Harbour was mooted, although in the event only the route from Carlisle via Newton Stewart succumbed. A 'Black 5' 4-6-0 No 44900 awaits departure with, on the right, an InterCity DMU and a 204hp diesel shunter.
G. S. Robinson

Left:
Even the mighty fell to the cutter's torch. Withdrawn 'King' class 4-6-0s of the GWR await their fate at Swindon on 26 May 1963. No 6011 *King James I* minus tender stands back to back with No 6018 *King Henry VI*. *P. J. Lynch*

Below left:
Diesels were instrumental in the operation of the long-distance Cliffe (Kent) to Uddingston (Glasgow) cement block train. BRCW Type 3 No D6555 of the Southern Region was photographed approaching York on 8 June 1963. *P. J. Lynch*

Above:
Gresley 'A3' class Pacific No 60103 was soon to make a name for itself as No 4472 *Flying Scotsman* when it was sold out of BR service in 1963. In its final BR form with German type smoke deflectors, the locomotive is seen passing York with an up express on 18 August 1962. *P. J. Lynch*

Right:
The English Electric Type 3 diesel-electrics were to prove their worth against all comers as the years went by. On 24 August, a remarkable formation includes No D6811, Pullman Car *Eunice* and ex-LNWR TPO No 30209 as part of the 17.30 Scarborough-Swindon. *P. J. Lynch*

Below right:
The SR/BR-designed diesel locomotives were withdrawn in December 1963. No 10203 was built in 1954 and later transferred to work on the LMR. No 10203 is seen here at Derby MPD on 30 June 1963, six months prior to withdrawal. Final scrapping did not take place until 1968. *N. E. Preedy*

1964

'What first looked like a step nearer a Channel Tunnel seemed more like a diffident shuffle, such were the financial and technical qualifications with which Mr Marples (Minister of Transport) hedged his statement . . . At least eight years will pass, it seems, before the Channel Tunnel is finished' — *Modern Railways* editorial.

Right:
The most costly single disaster in railway history occurred when fire destroyed Bishopsgate Goods Warehouse on the morning of 5 December 1964. Firemen hose down the remains of the depot the same evening.
L. Sandler

XP64

The Design Panel was created by the BTC in 1956 'to advise on the best means of obtaining a high standard of appearance and amenity in the design of its equipment'. Too late to wield much influence on the many Modernisation Plan purchases, the Panel made a major impact with its 'Carriage of Tomorrow' project.

This exercise started from a review of the 14 experimental coaches built in 1957. A specification was drawn up for a new carriage design which would be suitable for quantity production, as this was emphatically not a prestige train project. A primary restriction was the need to use the dimensions of the existing body shell and, in second class vehicles, to provide 64 seats although this was later rescinded. Mock-ups were shown to the public at a well-attended exhibition held at the Design Centre in London in March 1963.

From there, to production models. Although the integral coach was coming, the XP64 train as it was adventurously titled used standard Mk 1 underframes, with a fairing on the solebars to give a different 'look'. The eight Derby-built coaches consisted of three first class 42-seat corridor coaches (M13407-9), two second class 48-seat corridor coaches (M25508-9), and three second class 64-seat open coaches (M4727-9). All featured improved bodies, better thermal and acoustic insulation, new toilets, wider (5ft) double glazed windows, wider doors and bigger vestibules, and better lighting.

A particularly interesting feature was the external door arrangement. Because of the wish to widen doors from the standard 1ft 11½in, these were replaced by doors giving a clear opening of 2ft 11¼in and allowing easier boarding and alighting with luggage. Unfortunately, the design of one large and one small door hinged together on the jackknife principle proved both draughty and difficult to open; they were replaced in 1970. The designers considered it necessary to have a centre door, but this left room for only one other if unacceptable reductions in seating capacity were to be avoided. The result was a rather unsatisfactory staggered arrangement (see diagram), which was not perpetuated.

Below:
A design element which was not perpetuated, at least for the Mk 2 construction programme, was the unidirectional seating pattern. It is demonstrated here, with typical (?) reading material for second class passengers. *BR*

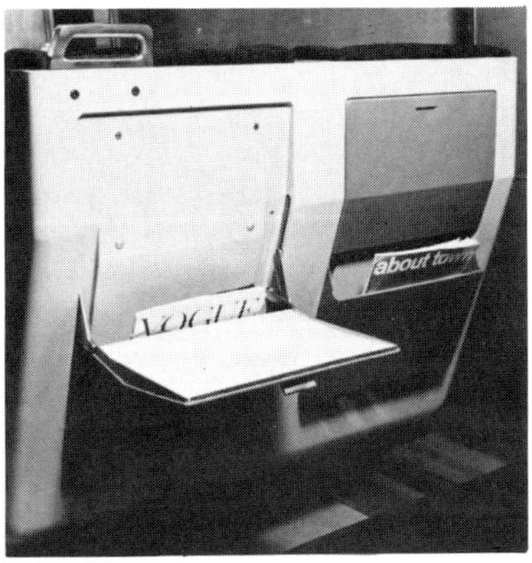

Bottom:
The XP64 'train of tomorrow' open second No M4727, as-built by Derby with folding doors. *BR*

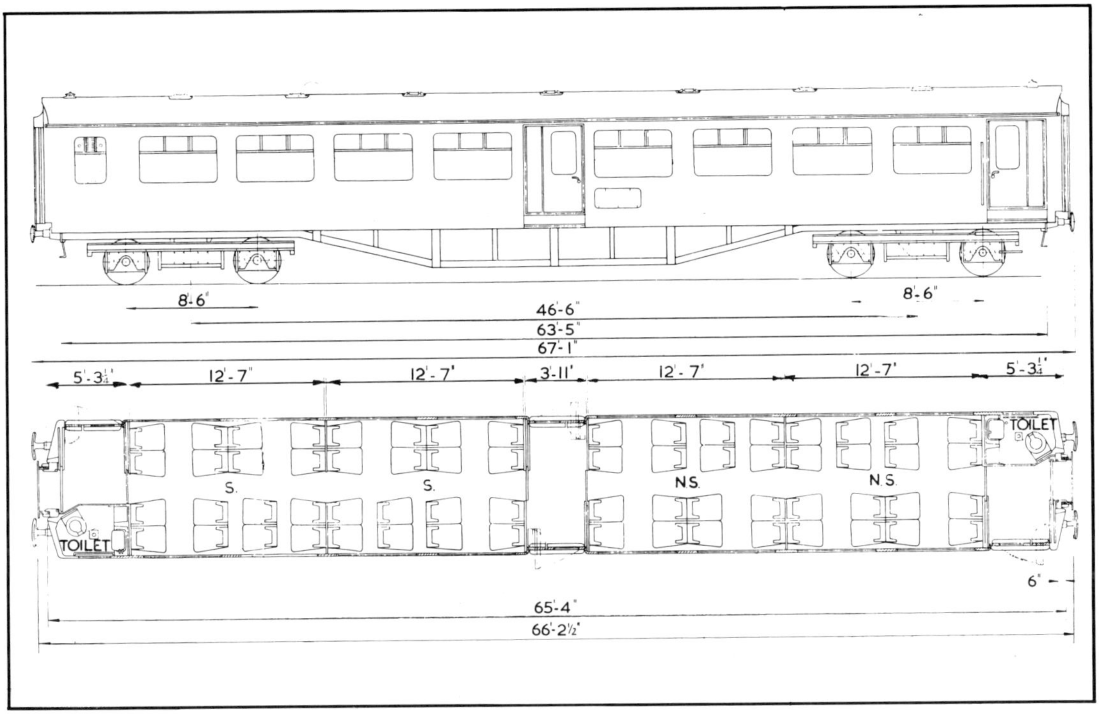

The door problem was solved eventually with the Mk 2b designs of 1967.

It was the second class open vehicles which offered the greatest design advances, especially in the seat shells made out of moulded fibreglass. Many of the features found their way into production models, though not the mixture of face-to-face and unidirectional seating. The toilet design was criticised harshly for its lack of space, and steps were taken to change this.

Together with some specially prepared standard Mk 1 stock, the train was set to work in summer 1964 as the Edinburgh-based 'Talisman' set, making a daily 786-mile round trip. From there it went to the West Riding trains, then to the Euston-Heysham service, and finally to the Western Region. The coaches were withdrawn by 1981, but examples of each have been preserved.

Below:
The public were allowed to inspect the train at Marylebone. *BR*

Derby Research

The new laboratories of BR's Engineering Research Division at Derby were opened by HRH The Duke of Edinburgh on 14 May. Their work had three objectives, dictated by the developing demands of the modern railway for higher speeds, more intensive utilisation of equipment, automation, reliable and shock-free transits of freight, and better comfort for the passenger and soundproofing of the vehicles. These objectives were:

- to obtain a better knowledge of the factors behind ideal equipment design;
- to cheapen the manufacture and maintenance costs of vehicles, but at the same time improve their reliability; and
- to study for the future completely new ideas in railway equipment and operation.

Of particular interest in 1964 was the research being carried out into the design of marshalling yards employing the Dowty Automatic Wagon Control instead of orthodox retarders. Already adopted for the new Tinsley, Sheffield yard, it was also to be installed at Scunthorpe and Bescot, and possibly added to existing yards to improve the control of wagons after they had passed through the retarders in the hump area.

The Dowty apparatus was essentially a series of hydraulic units, known as booster-retarders, laid on the inside of each running rail. The flanges of a passing vehicle depressed a hammer-headed plunger in each unit; the speed of that depression governed whether the unit offered resistance to the wheel (slowing down a vehicle making too high a speed) or provided thrust on the

Below:
Brunel's Saltash bridge was built in 1859, and is the only rail link between Devon and Cornwall. Great concern had been expressed over its structural soundness, but happily it was possible to dispel doubts. *P. J. Lynch*

up-stroke (accelerating a vehicle that was passing too slowly). The advantages of the Dowty Control were not only that it bid to limit the damage to freight and the heavy wagon repair bill resulting from marshalling shocks, because of its fine control of shunted wagon speed up to the point of impact with other wagons already occupying a yard siding, but also that it economised in marshalling yard construction, since it needed a less steeply graded hump. At Tinsley the economies were considerable, but elsewhere it would depend on the site.

The work at Derby consisted of computer calculations to decide the ideal location pattern of booster-retarders in a yard to maintain adequate clearances between wagon cuts of varying rollability as they descended from the hump, and thus to ensure satisfactory operation of the route-setting controls between cuts, and also to maintain steady progress of the stiffest-running vehicle right down a siding. Alas, the eclipse of the traditional hump yard in a few years was not perceived.

Other studies included:

- the effects of vibrations on freight and passengers;
- the thermal efficiency of refrigerating vehicles;
- the use of radar to detect hazards in the path of trains;
- the strength testing of integral coach body shells;
- the riding characteristics of freight vehicles;
- the performance and interaction of brakes, buffers and couplings;
- the fatigue stress in locomotive frames;
- the evolution of an optimum track structure;
- the wear and failure of rails;
- the effects on track and bridges of future motive power and vehicle developments.

Below left:
Over 2,000 Pallet Vans (Palvans) were built before it was discovered that they were unstable at speed when wear had set in. This caused their speed to be restricted and then to be withdrawn from traffic due to the incidence of freight train derailments. In 1962 there were no such problems, as 'J27' 0-6-0 No 65894 calls at Rowntrees sidings on the Foss Islands branch, York, to detach a train of them. *P. J. Lynch*

Below:
The Dowty units as installed at Tinsley marshalling yard, Sheffield. *BR*

Cartic

In the search for new traffics which might profitably be carried by rail, that of new cars from factories or docksides to distributors was considered. Although the Carflat wagons — old carriage underframes decked over — were cheap to produce, the carrying capacity was limited, while the 'tiered car vans' (TCV) of the Eastern Region with their twin decks between the bogies and internal lifts were far too costly and time-consuming to load.

Was there a double-deck alternative within the British loading gauge? Cars were becoming lower slung compared with a few years previously. Detailed examination of the private cars then on the market showed that the answer was yes, provided that some care was taken in what went where. The outcome was a twin-deck four-section articulated vehicle, with the lower deck rising over the bogies but maintaining a clearance of 4ft 10½in throughout. Above, the upper deck followed the contours of the lower, and vehicles up to 5ft 1in could be tolerated, except perhaps at the extremes of the sloping ends. The Cartic 4 was designed in consultation with Ford, whose entire model range could be accommodated.

Simultaneous and fast loading of both decks was possible, given some form of ramping for the upper deck and end loading for the lower. It was soon found that an old coaching underframe could be adapted to provide a mobile ramp. The intention was to operate trains of five or more vehicle sets, each of which was 203ft 5in long. Between 24 and 34 cars could be carried on each set, depending on their size. Cars were secured by a simple scotch pegged into the vehicle decking.

Speeds of 75mph were ensured, making the Cartics suitable also for car-carrier and car-sleeper services which conveyed private vehicles and their passengers, although they were not initially used in this manner. In service the Cartics were successful, although their totally open nature invited vandalism by stone-throwing from the lineside, and much trouble was caused by oil discharges from

Right:
Car-carrying trains using Carflats (converted passenger stock) allow up to five small cars to be loaded. Three lines of new Hillman Imps are shown at Johnstone, ready to be assembled into a 20-wagon train for movement to Gosford Green, Coventry. *BR*

Left:
Commercial vehicles, because of their height, can only be transported on single deck vehicles. Two per Carflat is the most that could be achieved on this southbound train from Bathgate seen here passing Gorebridge behind ex-LNER 'B1' class 4-6-0s Nos 61191 and 61324 in November 1964.
W. J. V. Anderson

diesel locomotives coating cars at the front of the train. Subsequent modifications included some wire mesh protection, and leading vehicles were equipped with plastic 'hoods', or a spare van took the place next to the locomotive.

The first commercial use was for Ford traffic, and the vehicles were privately owned. Ford had already become one of BR's largest customers, chartering over 60 trains a week, with regular components runs between factories at Dagenham and Halewood. These were supplemented by trains for finished cars which also served Bathgate and, later, Wakefield and Swansea as well. Cartics were deployed on Motorail trains for the first time in 1966 on the London-Perth route; at that time Motorail was the fastest growing part of the passenger business.

Below:
The Cartic 4 was the elegant solution, and the prototype unit was photographed at Swindon on 20 September 1964. *Brian Stephenson*

Merry-go-Round

If the train was to be the basic unit of movement, and the new traction was capable with 1,000 tons plus of trailing load, the railway could become a very cheap mover of materials passing in large quantities. Coal consigned from pits to power stations was an obvious contender for such treatment; what would be needed to translate this into practice?

One of the most unsatisfactory aspects of coal movement by rail was that of wagon provision, where whole fleets of costly wagons made as few as 20 loaded journeys a year. If a locomotive could be attached to a set of wagons on a semi-permanent basis, and the loading and discharging arrangements would allow, continuous operation could be achieved. That raised three big 'ifs', of which the wagon proved the easiest to solve.

The wagon design, known initially as HOP AB was an 18ft 3in wheelbase 26/32 ton capacity hopper, for which the initial orders were 1,880. Galvanised interiors, rounded corners, improved valley angles and six bottom doors extended virtually the whole width of the wagon combined to give a major advance in discharging techniques. Standard equipment was air braking, roller bearings and Instanter couplers. Lineside apparatus was to engage fitments on the wagon for automatic discharge whilst the train moved forward to a steady ½mph. Special slow speed control was fitted to certain of the Brush Type 4 locomotives in order for this to be achieved.

At the receiving end, the Central Electricity Generating Board were content to design new base load coal-fired power stations, initially at West Burton, Ferrybridge, Eggborough, Ratcliffe on Soar, Fidler's Ferry and Cottham, to accept the Merry-go-Round (MGR) method of working as it had become known. Modifications to allow MGR type loading were made to Drakelow C, Thorpe Marsh, Ironbridge B and Aberthaw B. 1964 saw an important advance, with a long-term agreement between the CEGB and the BRB for the conveyance of coal. Each power station was planned to need up to 20,000 tons a day, and apparatus

Left:
Electronic control apparatus at Ferrybridge C power station counts the series of MGR wagons and moves the lineside opening machines in and out automatically in a predetermined sequence. *BR*

for unloading was to be capable of handling trains with a payload of up to 2,000 tons. The contract was expected to double the amount of power station coal on rail to 60 million tons a year by 1970, of which 75% would be moving in block trains of high capacity wagons. The agreement also made possible the siting of power stations away from the coalfields and nearer the consuming areas; the later Didcot site involved the carriage of coal for 120 miles.

Less fortunate were the arrangements at the producing end. The National Coal Board refused to modify its existing pithead installations to suit MGR working with the new wagons other than at BR's expense. While the NCB was prepared to design the loading plant at the handful of new collieries to suit the railway, alterations at existing pits were turned down on the grounds that many of the new power stations would need to be fed by a number of collieries to get the right mix of fuel types, and that anyway it was the railway which stood to benefit, not the NCB. The dispute remained unsettled for a number of years, finally being resolved in the Coal Board's favour.

Left:
A merry-go-round train from Treeton Colliery with a Brush Type 4 locomotive in charge. Locomotives used regularly on MGR duties are fitted with slow speed control which enables them to proceed at a steady 0.5mph during the loading and unloading processes. *BR*

1964

Top right:
Electrification and dieselisation between them rendered the Stanier Pacifics surplus by 1964, and thought was given to transferring 11 of them to the Southern for use on the Bournemouth line. Clearance problems meant that the idea was not pursued, and the locomotives were scrapped. No 46250 *City of Lichfield* leaves Carlisle with the up 'Royal Scot' in December 1963.
A. R. Thompson

Above right:
Meanwhile, Southern Bulleid Pacifics were still working regular sorties into what had become WR territory. With a Bulleid coach in Western Region-lined maroon, unrebuilt 'West Country' 4-6-2 No 34099 *Lynmouth* leaves Honiton tunnel en route to Seaton Junction with a local from Exeter on 5 September 1964. *Paul Riley*

Right:
Newly delivered 0-6-0 diesel-hydraulic No D9505 passes Bristol Barrow Road engine sheds on 26 September 1964 with 'Hall' class 4-6-0 No 4919 *Donnington Hall* in the foreground. With the disappearance of the local freight work for which they were intended, the 'D95XX' class was obsolete before it was delivered, and all 56 were withdrawn within five years of the first locomotive appearing. *R. E. Toop*

Left:
Diesel traction did not mean increased reliability as a matter of course. Unfamiliar traction for both train crew and maintenance staff, coupled with some design faults, resulted in scenes such as this. 2-6-2T No 4100 pilots Sulzer No D162 on the 07.30 Newcastle-Paignton after the latter had failed at Cheltenham on 15 August 1964.
P. J. Lynch

Below left:
Perhaps the least satisfactory of all the pilot scheme main line diesels were the North British-built 'D600' class of five locomotives. No D601 *Ark Royal* enters Bodmin Road on 27 August 1964 with the 09.15 Plymouth to Penzance. All were withdrawn in 1967.
P. J. Lynch

Below:
Progress on the principal, or perhaps only, main line electrification scheme continued. By August 1964 the overhead was to be seen in the London area as 'Britannia' Class 7MT No 70044 *Earl Haig* nears Kenton with the up 'Lakes Express'. *P. J. Lynch*

Above:
The prototype Mk 2 coach was built in 1963 with the first production vehicles entering service in 1964. This corridor First No 13403 was one of a batch allocated to the Southern. It is seen at a later date in the 1964 corporate identity livery.
K. P. Lawrence

Right:
The Western Region's new diesel depot at Cardiff was opened in September 1964. This interior photograph shows the maintenance shed. The locomotive nearest the camera, Brush Type 4 No 1744, was introduced in June of the same year. *BR*

Below:
Handbills had yet to show any sign of sophistication.

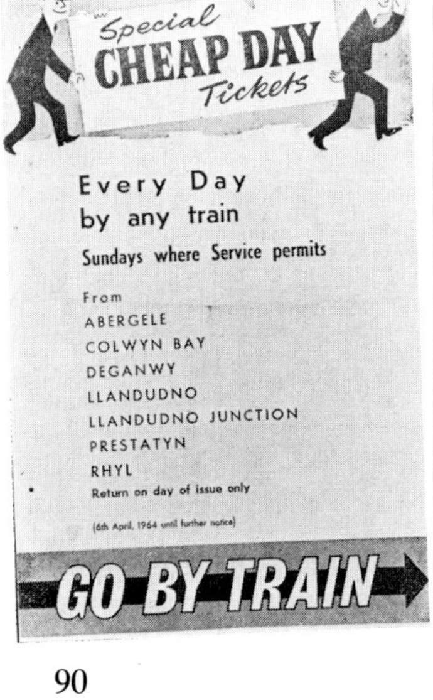

1965

'To a great extent the future of British Railways depends on what the travelling public and industry think of us' — Dr Beeching.

Below:
The spread of colour light signalling was marked by powerboxes springing up around the country. The new box at the south end of Wolverhampton High Level was to be commissioned shortly when this photograph was taken in March 1965. *BR*

Corporate Identity

The corporate identity programme was launched at the beginning of the year, the most immediately noticeable feature being the adoption of the title British Rail and the new symbol. The latter generated much comment. According to one source:

'The symbol is based upon the idea of two-way traffic movement. It can also be interpreted as rail tracks, and the arrows combine to produce an electrification flash. With an easily recognisable, forceful and simple outline, it can be reproduced in a wide range of materials and sizes without losing its impact'.

Another commentator felt that:

'A powerful suggestion of nervous energy in the crude vitality of its arrowheads begin to grow on one, and after all, anything would be an improvement on the previous heraldic abortion'.

At last, an attempt was being made to get away from the steam railway image which had been perpetuated in the unexciting finishes applied to much of the modernisation equipment. The programme was based upon the belief that, properly planned and

Below:
First manifestation of a blue colour scheme for locomotives was applied to No D1733 of the Brush Type 4s for the XP64 train. Subsequently, a darker shade was chosen for general usage but the overall effect was very similar. No D1733 was photographed at Derby Works. *P. H. Wells*

applied, good industrial design could act as a powerful but inexpensive selling agent.

One of the problems was the multiplicity of activities of the Railways Board. Not only rolling stock, but locomotives, stations, typefaces, uniforms, signposting, publicity etc, etc were all to be treated to a house style approach. The colours were to be monastral blue, pearl grey and flame red, none of which corresponded to any of the traditional Regional colours which in themselves had little meaning anyway. To ensure that both the policy and the way to apply it were understood, a design manual 'rule book' was produced.

An important consideration was the appearance of the livery on trains, especially after suffering wear and tear with age. The blue was thought to provide a fresh appearance under most conditions, although the initial proposal to keep the blue and grey livery for InterCity use only was progressively abandoned. In practice, the matt blue applied at the outset quickly took on a tatty look, and a glossier finish was substituted with much improved results.

Speed of application was limited in view of the expense. Generally, the scheme would be applied with planned repainting or renovation, although new items were to be so treated at the start. It was hoped that sufficient would be done to have an impact on the public by the end of the year, emphasising visually the progress towards a unified, efficient and viable railway system.

Below:
The appearance of a few of the remaining pre-nationalisation designs in the corporate livery was short-lived as most were then being quickly withdrawn. Brake Second No M27001M was one of the few coaches thus treated, though parcels vans survived much longer and were painted accordingly. *BR*

The Trunk Routes Report

The Mk 2 Beeching Report was published early in 1965. This time the spotlight was on the major through routes which, because of the competitive way in which the railway system was built, had more than an element of duplication about them. If, the argument went, the traffic on offer or likely to be on offer in the next 20 years could be carried on one of the routes, why maintain two? Better utilisation meant lower unit costs and a concentration of scarce investment funds where they would provide the maximum benefit. 'The real choice is between an excessive and increasingly uneconomic system, with a corresponding tendency for the railways as a whole to fall into disrepute and decay, or the selective development and intensive utilisation of a more limited trunk route system.'

When it came to the selection of routes, the tone of the Report was muted. The 'tablets of stone' approach had disappeared, to be replaced with reassuring noises that lack of selection did not necessarily imply closure, and that constructive criticism was welcomed. Worked examples in the best textbook fashion were given, and the list of criteria included capital expenditure needs, physical characteristics and network considerations. Thus the Trans-Pennine route via Diggle was marked down compared with the Calder Valley route on account of its stiffer gradients, relative lack of intermediate traffic (hard luck, Huddersfield!), and lack of a quick access to the West Coast main line via Copy Pit and Preston. Similarly, in the South Pennines, the Woodhead route was extolled for its modernity, directness, capacity and connections, while the ex-Midland Railway Hope Valley and Peak Forest lines were both beset by heavy maintenance costs and speed restrictions.

Below:
The Woodhead route had the necessary capacity, and what was more it had been comprehensively modernised relatively recently. A Manchester-Sheffield express behind No E26014 passes Godley Junction and meets No E26017 with an oil train taking the route for Warrington. *John Glover*

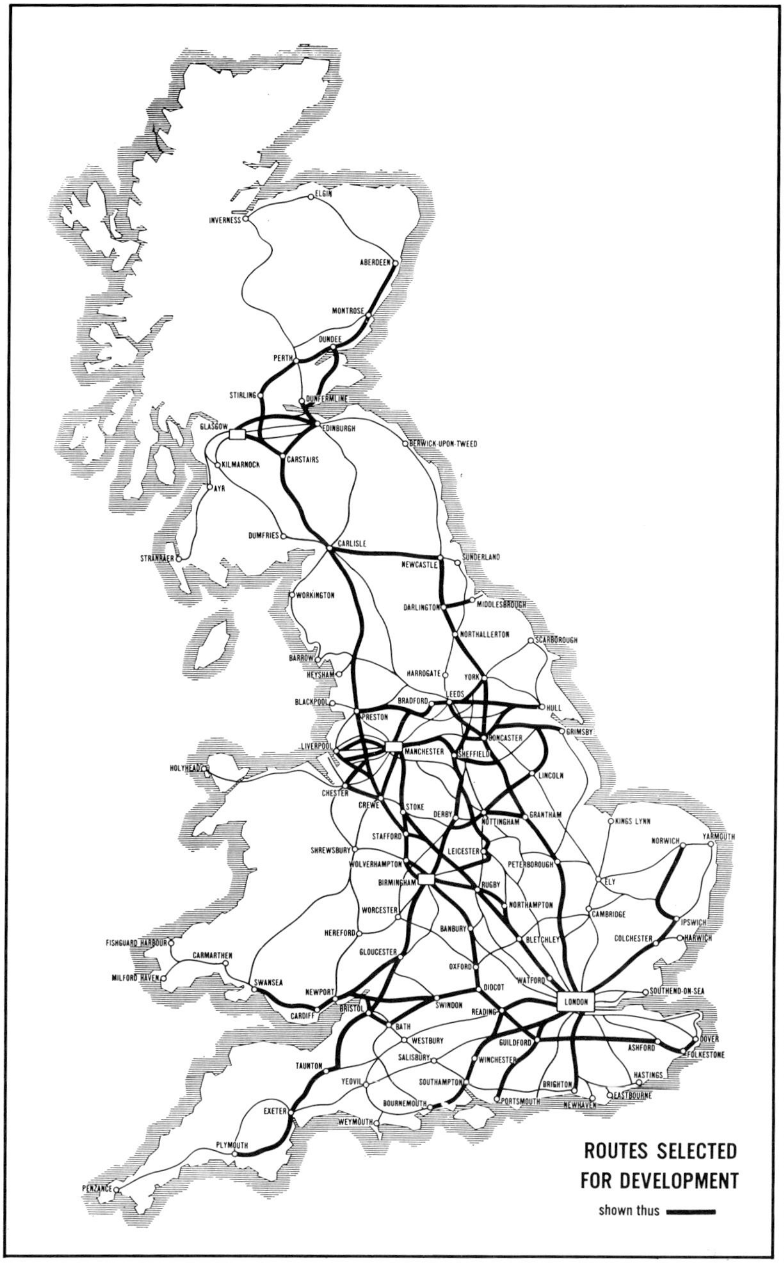

Dr Beeching departed from BR shortly afterwards; 10 years later as Lord Beeching he reflected upon his railway career in an interview with *The Times*:

'People often say to me, "What would you do if you had your time over again, aren't you sorry you did that or the other?" It may sound very smug and arrogant, but my answer is my only regret is that I didn't get further along the road that I chose in the time available. I haven't any regrets at all other that I didn't get more done.'

Electric Transmission versus Hydraulic

Below:
Chief diesel-hydraulic protagonist was the 'Western' class C-C locomotive of 2,700hp. An unidentified member of the class gets a long freight on the move out of Highbridge on a summer evening in 1965.
G. G. M. Robinson

Whilst both diesel-electric and diesel-hydraulic locomotives have been found entirely capable of running the railway, it was felt that two different transmission systems could not be continued indefinitely. Pre-modernisation, experience had been confined to seven main line locomotives, all with electric transmission; this was also favoured with the pilot scheme orders because of existing facilities and experience with comparable components in electric traction. The Western Region, however, had no electrics, and favoured hydraulic transmission partly because of observations made in West Germany, and partly to avoid the need to set up electrical maintenance facilities. There was also a decidedly better power/weight ratio, with D800 2,200hp 'Warship' diesels weighing 80 tons against a D200 2,000hp English Electric machine weighing 133 tons. Initially, 14 hydraulic locomotives were built.

Electric transmission uses a medium speed engine (800-900rpm) to generate an electric current, which then drives the dc traction motors. There is no physical connection between the engine and the driven axles, and this means that engine speed can be held constant irrespective of the running speed of the locomotive. Hydraulic transmission uses high-speed engines (1,500rpm) which, by means of hydraulic convertors, fluid couplings or convertor plus mechanical gearing provides a direct connection between the engine and the road wheels.

Performance and efficiency tests were carried out between locomotives in power categories 4 and 3, with the results shown in Table 1. On nearly every count the diesel-electrics showed an advantage; when it came to casualties, the hydraulics showed better results for electrical equipment of which they had little, but this was more than offset by poorer performance with engines

Table 1: Transmission types compared

Class	*D1500 (47)*	*D1000 (52)*	*D6700 (37)*	*D700 (35)*
Transmission	Electric	Hydraulic	Electric	Hydraulic
hp	2,750	2,700	1,750	1,700
Capital cost (£'000)	125	136	83	88
Weight (tons)	105.6	98.8	95.2	68.2
Average availability since new (%)	85.2	76.6	81.8	83.7
Average availability 1964 (%)	86.1	64.3	90.5	82.8
Miles/casualty since new	11,000	8,500	31,000	18,000
Casualties/locomotive 1964:				
Engine	0.75	1.08	0.16	0.24
Transmission	0.09	0.26	0.01	0.22
Electrical equipment	0 50	0.41	0.15	0.11
Totals	1.34	1.75	0.32	0.57

Table 2: Diesel-hydraulic locomotive summary

Total of introduction	*BR Class No*	*No series*	*Total built*	*hp*	*Last of class withdrawn*
1958	41*	D600-4	5	2,000	1967
1958	42/3	D800-70	71	2,200	1972
1959	22	D6300-57	58	1,100	1972
1961	35	D7000-100	101	1,700	1975
1961	52	D1000-73	74	2,700	1977
1964	14	D9500-55	56	650	1969

* Not actually allocated as system not introduced until after withdrawal.

(with diverse causes of failure), and transmissions (which suffered from under-design). Even their initial weight advantage turned against the hydraulics as they could not summon enough braking power to halt unfitted freight trains. When they were ordered, it was thought that the unfitted wagon would quickly disappear, but this was not to be. This led to the first major incursion of diesel-electrics to be based on WR territory, when English Electric Type 3 diesels (later Class 37) were sent to South Wales.

The investigation concluded that if each system was to be developed afresh, the overall differences would probably only be marginal. Despite having built 365 hydraulic transmission locomotives, they were in a small minority compared with the overall fleet; the decision was thus taken to standardise on electric transmission for future construction. The hydraulics soldiered on for a time, but the last main line locomotive of the type, No D1023 *Western Fusilier*, was withdrawn in February 1977.

Below:
The Class 3 power group was represented in the hydraulic camp by the Beyer Peacock 'Hymeks'. A brand-new No D7046 in works primer was ready to leave Derby on a trial run on 23 July 1962.
P. J. Lynch

Freightliners, but no Open Terminals

'The basic idea,' to quote the Reshaping Report, 'is to combine road and rail movement in such a way as to take advantage of the low cost of fast through train movement as the means of providing trunk haulage over medium to long distances, for flows of traffic which, though dense, are composed of consignments too small in themselves to justify through train operation, and to do so without the disadvantages of either costly assembly of trains by wagon load movement on rail, or costly transfer of merchandise between road and rail vehicles.'

The method was to be fast scheduled trains of flat wagons which would convey containers of 8ft×8ft cross-section in modular lengths of up to 30ft. Fifty-five special terminals equipped with transfer cranes would be opened to feed and link the services, and the expensively modernised marshalling yards were to be bypassed completely. Part of the traffic was expected to be diverted from unremunerative wagon load and sundries consignments, but some passenger-rated parcels traffic was also thought to be a candidate. Together, these totalled 14 million tons a year, to which an estimated 16 million tons of road-borne traffic was confidently expected to be added. The report waxed lyrical about the financial prospects for the railways, but added an important caveat that it would not be British Railways' wish or intention to carry out all collection and delivery. It was expected that many customers

Below:
The prototype liner train equipment was based upon a wagon length of 42ft 6in, and was designed to carry up to four 10ft modules. Ideas developed, and in production rather longer vehicles of 62ft 6in were built, allowing six standard modules per wagon. *BR*

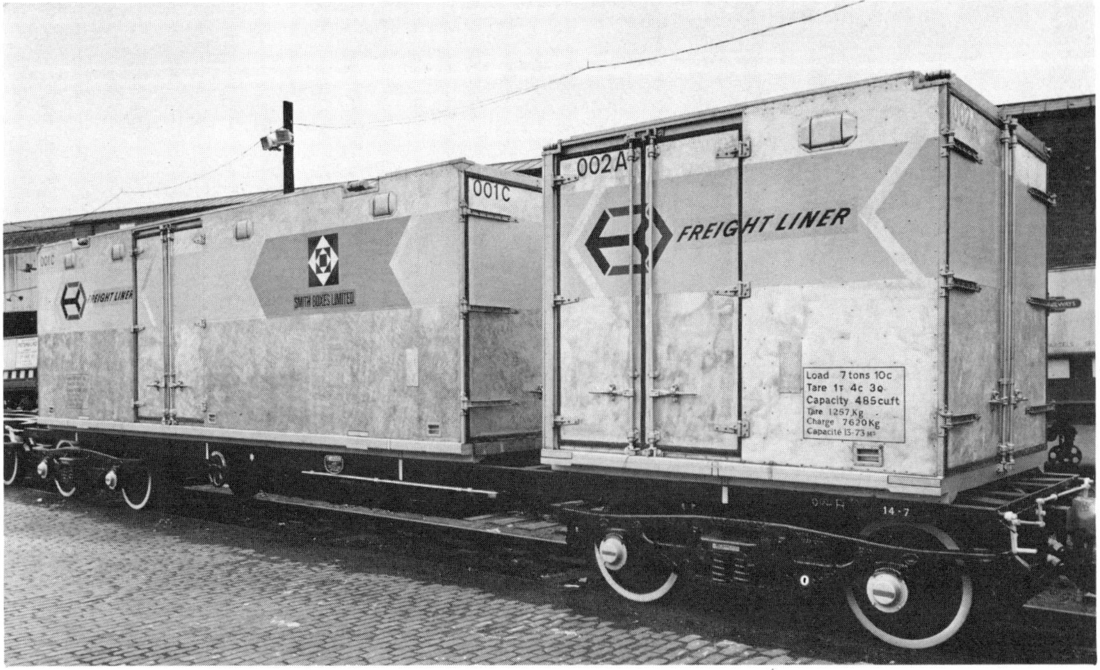

Left:
Leaflet advertising the new services to and from Liverpool (Garston).

would prefer to use their own vehicles. Some indeed would be hauliers, who it was hoped might subcontract the trunk haul to the railway.

It was this principle of open terminals which provoked the opposition of the National Union of Railwaymen, whose cartage members feared redundancy. For months there was no headway made despite alternate threats and promises by the Board. Wagons were built and terminals prepared at London (Maiden Lane) and Glasgow (Gushetfaulds) in 1964, but it was not until November 1965 that commercial loads were carried, and then only with BR vehicles allowed in the terminals. A London-Manchester service was started in February 1966, but only four containers on the 15-wagon train were loaded. Slowly the services were expanded and traffic grew; by May the Glasgow service carried its first full trainload. August saw the 10,000th container, by which time 550 were being carried weekly. Garston and Aberdeen terminals were added by the end of the year.

The question of terminal access was finally resolved on 2 March 1967 after Government intervention. The Labour Minister of Transport, Mrs Barbara Castle, was understood to have threatened to put a stop on further investment unless the NUR withdrew its ban, which had been in operation for nearly three years. The Board, at last, got their way.

1965

Right:
1965 saw the general adoption of the 24hr clock on the railways. Whilst timetables became much less prone to misinterpretation, there was the occasional odd result such as the adaptation which had to be carried out to this venerable L&Y wooden train departure indicator at Rochdale. *John Glover*

Below:
The funeral train of Sir Winston Churchill was hauled from Waterloo to Handborough after the funeral at St Paul's Cathedral on 30 January. The train locomotive was SR 'Battle of Britain' class No 34051 *Sir Winston Churchill*. The train was photographed approaching Richmond.
P. J. Lynch

Above:
Steam at Paddington was latterly confined to the 16.15 to Banbury. On the last occasion in 'normal' service for Paddington steam, 'Castle' class 4-6-0 No 7029 *Clun Castle* passes Westbourne Park on 11 June 1965. The usual four coaches had to be strengthened to nine.
P. J. Lynch

Left:
Almost unbelievably, 'Manor' class 4-6-0 No 7816 *Frilsham Manor* retained a GWR appellation on the tender to the end. Photographed behind Horton Road shed at Gloucester on 16 December 1965, the lettering could still be made out. *P. J. Lynch*

Below left:
A 20-year agreement was signed with road-haulier Tartan Arrow in October, which provided for a nightly chartered train between Kentish Town and Bridgeton. A London-Glasgow journey time of 10-14 hours was promised. Trains were painted in the red and white of the company's colours, like this covered carriage truck (CCT).
L. Williams

Above:
There were still 58 sites available for Camping Coaches, from Golspie in the north to Corfe Castle in the south. Travelling by rail was a condition of hire.

Above right:
A 10-year contract was signed with Scottish Malt Distillers in December for the carriage of 70,000+ tons of barley and malt annually from East Anglia. The traffic started in spring 1966 in the privately owned vans of which 100 were built by Powell Duffryn. Vacuum rather than air brakes were fitted. *Ian Allan Library*

Right:
A Day Rail Rover between Edinburgh, Stirling, Perth and Dundee gave rather more scope than would be the case today.

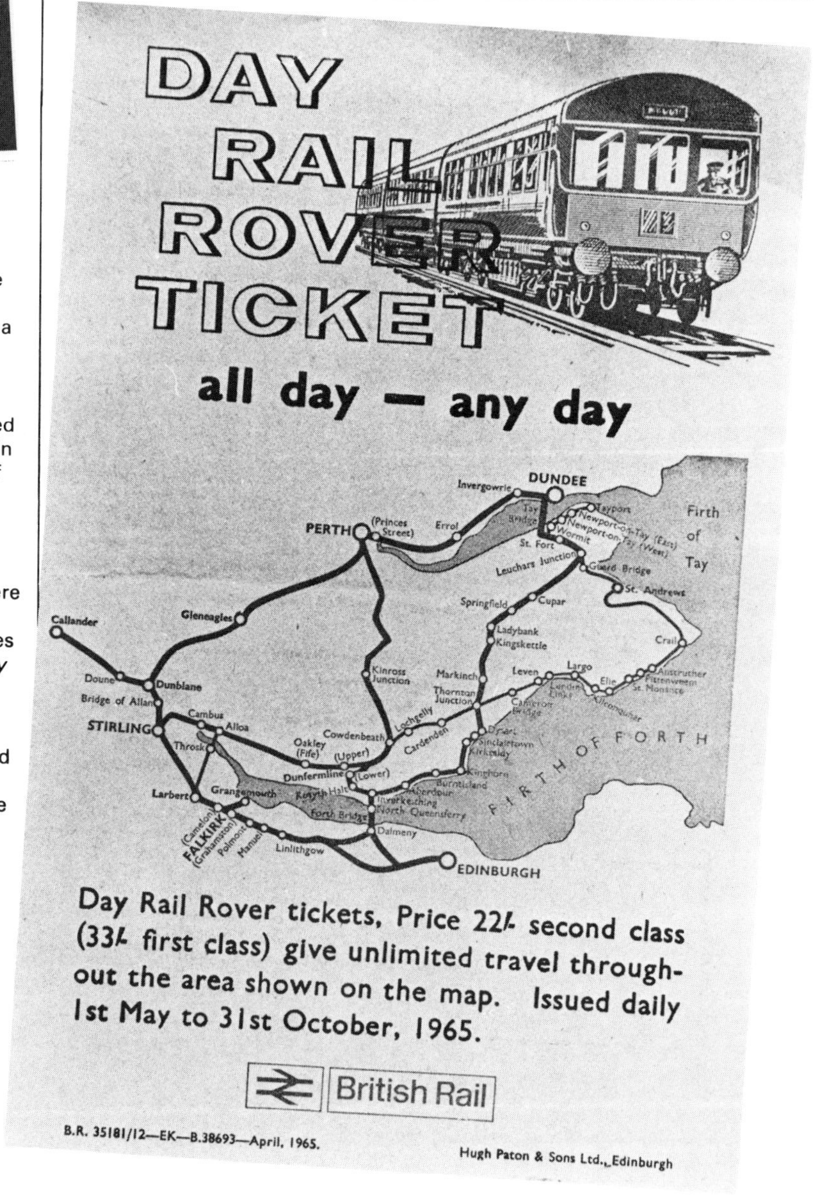

1966

'Modern machines are revolutionising maintenance methods on the permanent way. By the end of 1966, only two years after the new techniques had been introduced, they had spread over 72% of British Railways' running lines. During that time, permanent way manpower was cut by nearly a quarter, from 23,350 to 17,700. There were incentive schemes for nearly all the remaining staff' — BRB Annual Report and Accounts.

Right:
The Eastern Region introduced 'BRUTE' circuit working in East Anglia. Here, two railwaymen find a considerable effort is needed to load the train at Liverpool Street on 30 September 1966. Pushing BRUTES out of a van without using a ramp, though tempting, was strictly forbidden as it had a good chance of destroying the vehicle footboards. *BR*

Electrics at Euston

The day some said would never come: 18 April 1966 saw the full electric timetable introduced for the Manchester and Liverpool electrification, a decade after work started on the scheme.

It is perhaps kinder to draw a veil over the years of disrupted train services which resulted from the interminable engineering works, remarking only that the lessons were learnt the hard way and applied on subsequent occasions. At least, if the services had been so awful before, they would be perceived as all the better by the public now that work was completed.

And indeed the services were excellent. Star billing went to the Euston-Manchester/Liverpool services, each on a basic two-hourly headway. Journey times were cut by up to one-third, with a number of trains averaging over 70mph for the throughout journey including stops. From the start the new timetable proved highly attractive. Significant increases were made in loadings and revenue, much new business being generated by the accelerated timings. Among the services were eight daily Pullmans, using new air-conditioned stock. Completing the journey to Manchester or Liverpool in less than 2hr 40min, they set new standards of luxury and convenience.

Anglo-Scottish and other long-distance services also benefited by the faster timings over the electrified section between Euston and Crewe. Average accelerations on weekdays between London and Glasgow were 43min by day service and 80min overnight in the down direction, and 53 and 64min respectively in the up direction. Services linking the Midlands and northwest with

Below:
The squarer front profile distinguishes the later AL6 locomotives built for the extension of electrification to Euston. No E3169 receives attention in the District Electric Depot at Willesden.
John Glover

Table 1: Shortest Schedule times from and to Euston

Town	*Distance miles*	*Time down min*	*Speed mph*	*No runs daily*	*Time up min*	*Speed mph*	*No runs daily*
Rugby	84.55	66	75.0	7	66	75.0	7
Coventry	93.95	73	77.0	2	80	70.3	1
Stafford	133.55	106	75.6	2	105	76.3	1
Stoke-on-Trent*	149.80	140	64.2	1	140	64.2	3
Crewe	158.00	121	78.3	6	119	79.7	2
Manchester	183.90	156	72.7	2	155	73.1	1
Liverpool	193.75	155	75.0	1	155	75.0	1
Preston†	209.00	191	65.7	1	196	64.0	1
Morecambe†	234.00	216	65.0	1	277	61.8	1
Holyhead†	263.70	256	61.8	1	260	60.8	1
Carlisle†	299.10	276	65.0	1	279	64.3	1
Glasgow†	401.40	395	61.0	1	390	61.8	1

* Diesel-hauled from Stafford.

† Diesel-hauled north of Crewe.

Source: *Modern Railways*, March 1966, p128.

Scotland were also speeded up. Trains between Euston and Birmingham were accelerated with electric traction introduced as far as Coventry, although the West Midlands and the Potteries had to wait until 1967 for the full benefits to reach them. Likewise, only Wolverhampton enjoyed electric services from the Midlands to the north. A regular service operated by electric multiple-units

Table 2: Specimen working times — 07.50 Euston-Manchester (Pullman)

Distance (miles)			*hr min*
0.00	Euston	dep	0.00
5.40	Willesden Junction	pass	0.07½
17.45	Watford Junction	arr	0.17
		dep	0.18
31.65	Tring	pass	0.29
46.65	Bletchley	pass	0.39
62.85	Blisworth	pass	0.50
82.55	Rugby	pass	1.05½
97.10	Nuneaton	pass	1.16½
110.00	Tamworth	pass	1.25½
127.15	Colwich	pass	1.37
133.55	Stafford	pass	1.44
158.00	Crewe	pass	2.02
162.60	Sandbach	pass	2.11½
176.90	Wilmslow	pass	2.21½
183.00	Stockport	arr	2.27
		dep	2.28
188.90	Manchester	arr	2.37

Schedule incorporates 3min recovery time, 1½min before Rugby and 1½min before Stafford.

Above:
First electric train into Euston was the 15.02 from Windermere on 22 November 1965. Train locomotive was No E3033. *M. Peach*

Right:
Part of a pamphlet extolling the new services. A poster version won an award in a competition sponsored by the Council of Industrial Design.

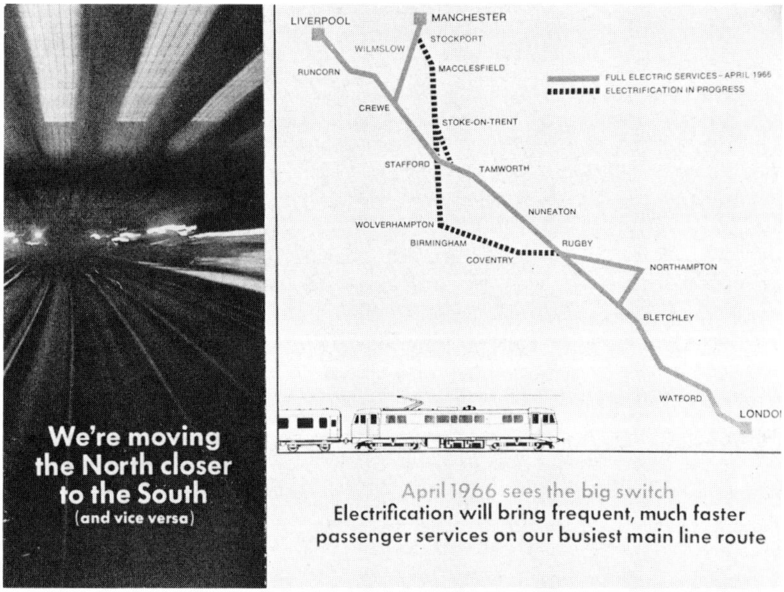

was also introduced between Euston, Bletchley, Rugby and Coventry.

To work these services, the first of the Mk 2 production vehicles were delivered, and sufficient coaches were turned out in the new blue and grey livery to make a respectable showing on the principal trains from the commencement of the timetable. The locomotive fleet was augmented by the building of 100 of the AL6 (later Class 86) design, which was intended to take account of all the lessons learned in the earlier batches, but which incorporated axle-hung traction motors that were subsequently found to play havoc with the track. On the local services, the AM10 (later Class 310) units were to reign supreme at the London end. Novel features were the integral construction and the fitting of disc brakes. Their superior passenger accommodation won them general customer approval.

The London Peak Problem

Three-quarters of all journeys on the railways' London commuter network were for work purposes, and this factor therefore dominated all aspects of the services and their finances. With Central London being by far the most popular destination, the maximum demand was concentrated into peak periods at the beginning and end of each working day. This resulted in massive under-utilisation at other times. From this certain conclusions were drawn:

- Capacity is entirely a peak problem.
- Off-peak demand can be met at marginal cost.
- Population and employment trends were major determinants of demand.
- General decline in carryings since 1961 had not affected rail's market share.

The pattern of demand around the Capital was by no means even. As the table shows, the lion's share of BR's carryings was that of the Southern Region, followed by the Eastern Region's Liverpool Street and Fenchurch Street lines. The other London termini carried only modest loads in comparison. However, the availability or otherwise of Underground services had much to do with this; thus London Transport's Northern line branches brought 26,000 passengers past Camden Town into the central area on the heaviest hour.

Overcrowding in the peak arose principally because the demands were so out of proportion to those arising at other times. Although total peak hour travel was declining, the pattern of usage was becoming more concentrated — there had been a 15% rise in passengers during the busiest hour on the Southern over the previous decade. Various ameliorative measures such as increasing trains to 10 cars on the South Eastern Division had been

Above:
A Holborn Viaduct-Sevenoaks train formed of 4-SUB units passes Loughborough Junction in South London.
Ian Allan Library

Above:
The Southern's attempt at a double-decker train resulted in the construction of the pair of 4-DD units. Loading gauge restrictions confined them to a handful of routes on the South Eastern Division. A peak working to Dartford via Bexleyheath was photographed leaving Cannon Street. *R. C. Riley*

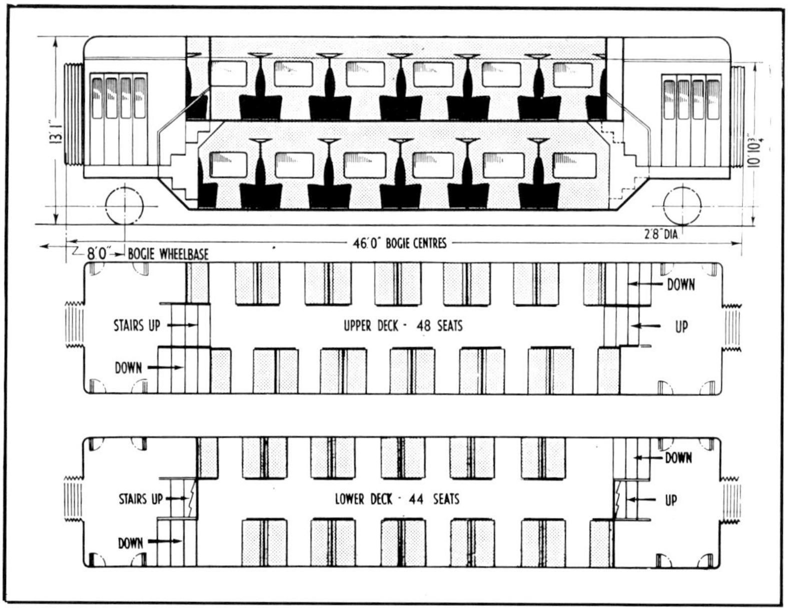

carried out over the years, but many stretches of track near the terminals were supporting the absolute maximum number of trains that modern signalling would permit. Nevertheless, the Southern planned to add 28,500 peak seats in the massively revamped, but as it turned out operationally unsound, 1967 timetable.

Meanwhile, the boffins revived the idea of the double-deck train. Using articulated stock on the Cartic 4 principle, it was possible to design vehicles to allow two saloons with 6ft headroom. Loading and unloading were to be through wide folding end doors with short stairways leading to each saloon from the vestibules. To allow free circulation, wide gangways and 2+2 seating were proposed, giving 92 seats per car, 44 lower and 48 upper deck. Car length was to be 46ft only, and 14 cars would equal a standard 10-car train in length. Although the 1,288 seating capacity was only 31% higher, the total carrying capacity would have allowed for 500 extra passengers without overcrowding. This represented an effective gain of about 40%.

'Heaviest hour' arrivals in Central London, 1966

		1,000s	*% by Region*
ER	Fenchurch Street	19	
	Liverpool Street	40	
	King's Cross	2	
			22
LMR	Broad Street	2	
	St Pancras	5	
	Euston	6	
	Marylebone	5	
			6
WR	Paddington	8	
			3
SR	Waterloo/Vauxhall	48	
	Victoria	39	
	London Bridge/Waterloo East/ Charing Cross/Cannon Street	86	
	Elephant & Castle/Blackfriars/ Holborn Viaduct	17	
			69
		277	100

Note: A further 232,000 arrived by Underground.

Above:
This view taken from the top of the Shell Building shows the approaches to Waterloo's 21 platforms. Should there be a points failure or derailment at anytime chaos will result. A rebuilt 'Merchant Navy' is arriving with an up Bournemouth train whilst a Standard Class 4 2-6-4T acts as one of the station pilots.
R. Jackson

The Basic Railway

The railway traditionally operated a uniform policy on pricing, ticket sales, documentation and accountancy. Yet the mere job of selling tickets was consuming as much as 5% of the total passenger revenue. Was it really necessary to treat the whole system the same, and in particular did a small station on a branch line need the same range of facilities as a principal inter-city station?

Eastern Region research suggested strongly that local, commuter and inter-city travel were three different markets. With local services, simplified systems could save costs and enable more resources to be directed to servicing the inter-city market. The King's Lynn-Hunstanton line was chosen as a guinea pig. The fares structure was replaced by a system of single fares only, themselves related both to comparable bus fares and to the previously widely used cheap day return facility. Station staff performing commercial duties were withdrawn, and all tickets were issued on the train by collector/guards. No through bookings were allowed, and any passengers travelling 'off-branch' rebooked at King's Lynn. Tickets for local travel were not to be sold even at King's Lynn booking office, and when applied to all local services this would lead to the evolution to a travel centre. The branch, meanwhile, became a self-contained railway.

This was only the first step. What other simplifications could be achieved? Rationalised train services with trains confined to the branch would ensure maximum utilisation of a predetermined number of train sets. Singling the line, minimising signalling and introducing automatic level crossings would all reduce the costs.

Below:
Unstaffing of stations became a bandwagon for all Regions. This public notice (in a decidedly non-corporate image typeface) referred to the intermediate stations on the Settle & Carlisle line.

Below right:
At Shepley & Shelley a Metro-Cammell DMU forms a Huddersfield-bound service from Sheffield. The station is unstaffed, but as yet remains in good repair.
G. G. M. Robinson

The number of stations at which a service could call economically would be related to the time which could be made available in the diagram rather than to the costs of maintaining the stations. Thus the concept of the basic railway emerged.

So far, so good, especially if revised methods of working could retain rather more railway than would otherwise be the case. Similar action took place all over East Anglia, and with variations elsewhere. However, some of the problems never seemed to be properly solved, due perhaps in some cases to injudicious union agreements:

- Forcing passengers to rebook *always* on through journeys was an unnecessary irritant, especially when travelling from a staffed station. (It was soon found out that exceptions had to be made for passengers holding travel warrants.)
- Automatic passing loops with sprung points, although part of the original planning, were not introduced.
- Loss of staff/customer contact at local stations, which was particularly trying when trains were running out of course or timetable displays had been vandalised. The provision of remote public address systems was not tackled.
- The interface between local and other trains was not satisfactorily resolved. For instance, on the East Suffolk, the retention of a through loco-hauled London service made insistence on rebooking at Ipswich a nonsense, while at manned stations operating a closed barrier system for other trains, how was the local passenger to gain access?
- Boarding up of disused buildings rather than demolition gave the railway an appearance of neglect.

Below:
A Derby Lightweight DMU leaves Thurston on a Cambridge-Ipswich local. Thurston, Elmswell, Kennet and Dullingham were proposed for closure but reprieved; by so doing receipts of £8,000 per year were retained and a bus subsidy of £3,000 a year was avoided, for the cost of about £1,000 for lighting and maintaining the stations and the fuel for restarting the trains. *John C. Baker*

Wagon Design

Reshaping meant rethinking the wagon fleet, and what it was meant to achieve. Generally, the British wagon had only a small capacity, was designed for modest speeds, and had a good chance of not being fitted with continuous brakes. The examination which took place was a combined effort between the marketing and engineering departments, with the permanent way and operating staffs contributing their points of view, and the research division adding a more fundamental approach.

The features looked for in a wagon by each member of the teams were not necessarily all compatible. Some of the considerations were as follows:

- The ratio of payload to tare weight needed to improve to 3:1 or more.
- The better the payload/tare ratio, the greater the suspension problems resulting from the difference between empty and loaded condition.
- Longer wagons reduce the tare weight as they require only one set of buffing gear, couplings and brakes.

Below:
First of the long-wheelbased BR-owned covered vans, the COV ABs, appeared about three years later as a result of the review. For the first time, British Rail could offer traders a van of a comparable size to those used for continental traffic. *L. Williams*

Right:
Internally, the vans could happily carry palletised products, in this case seven containing car body parts from the Austin Morris body works at Swindon to Longbridge. Note however the wasted space in the roof of the van, a factor which was later to lead to the abandonment of the carriage of BRUTES in trains. *BR*

- Long wagons have greater 'throwover' on curves, and this needs greater clearances, often a particular problem in private sidings.
- Railway modernisation had aimed at increasing clearances where possible.
- Technical infringements of the loading gauge might be acceptable for certain vehicle profiles on specified routes.
- Axle-loading restrictions may be eased by fitting costly bogies which also improve ride quality.
- Low centre of gravity improves stability and increases the height available for body construction or for carrying large containers, but small wheels lead to rail stress and braking problems.
- Specialised wagons risk low utilisation and becoming obsolete.
- Standard wagons may have their bodies adapted for different types of traffic, or on a larger scale, bodies may be interchangeable.
- A modern wagon which meets the stresses and strains of high-speed running may offer a physical life longer than the period for which it is economic to maintain it.
- Reducing the need to chain or sheet loads saves weight and speeds handling, but loads must be protected from damage to prevent claims and preserve goodwill.
- Commercial requirements are less likely to dictate high-speed than operating considerations, where a mix of very different train speeds may be unacceptable.
- Capital costs must be considered together with maintenance costs.
- Commercial requirements can advance research and development, for instance the 100-ton bogie tank wagon.
- Private ownership of wagons relieves the railway of many problems, and ties the customer to rail.

Such were the thoughts which went into the design of the modern wagon fleet. For new construction, air brakes were now standard, but many vacuum and unbraked wagons remained.

Below:
Bogie wagons of 100ton glw were popular, but research into riding of vehicles made the four-wheeler more competitive again. A train of new Metro-Cammell-built bogie cement wagons crosses the Thames on the West London line behind Class 47 No D1999. *BR*

1966

Right:
1966 saw the end of steam traction on the Isle of Wight and closure of all remaining lines except between Ryde Pier Head and Shanklin. The last surviving ex-LSWR Class 02 0-4-4T No W24 *Calbourne* takes water at the end of the platform at Pier Head station. *John Glover*

Below:
First of the Underground vehicles to be delivered arrives at Fishbourne on a Pickfords boat transporter on 2 September 1966. *BR*

Above:
The Great Central main line was closed from 5 September 1966, leaving for the time being the Nottingham-Rugby section to be served by six conductor-guard operated trains a day. Ashby Magna was one of the stations to be reprieved, and Stanier Class 5 4-6-0 No 45288 leaves a deserted station on 9 May with the 18.15 from Nottingham Victoria. *M. Mitchell*

Above left:
Closure came to the Somerset & Dorset Joint line. Ivatt Class 2 2-6-2T No 41242 waits at Evercreech Junction before departing with a train for Highbridge.
G. G. M. Robinson

Left:
A pair of 'AM10' electric units prepare to leave Coventry as the 21.55 to Bletchley on 6 October 1966. These units brought a new standard of passenger comfort to suburban electric services.
John Clarke

Right:
By 1966, most of the dwindling fleet of steam locomotives was on its last legs. 'J37' 0-6-0 No 64620 was pictured shunting at Inverkeithing on 26 August 1966, and survived long enough to be one of the last four, all withdrawn from Dundee the following year.
P. J. Lynch

Below:
The Scottish Region closed both St Enoch and Buchanan Street in Glasgow during 1966. This major rationalisation saved nearly £1m a year in operating costs alone, and released valuable sites for development. English Electric Type 4 No D365 arrives at Buchanan Street with the 09.30 from Aberdeen on 29 May 1965. *W. S. Sellar*

1967

'1967 was a bad year financially. Revenue fell considerably mainly because of the depressed state of the national economy, and although substantial savings in working costs were made the financial results were markedly worse than those for 1966. The deficit was £153 million, compared with £134.7 million for the previous year' — BRB Annual Report and Accounts.

Right:
Merger of the Eastern and North Eastern Regions took place from 1 January. The dish aerial on the top of the old NER headquarters building in York, seen here, is part of the first privately owned microwave radio-telephone system in Britain, installed in 1964 between York, Darlington and Newcastle. The building became the new combined ER HQ. *John Glover*

Labour Transport Policy

The Labour Government had no wish to pursue mass rail closures, and the programme slowed appreciably. By 1966, a major fault was seen in that 'the Board was given no proper yardstick . . . for measuring the effectiveness of the railway system . . . too little account had been taken in the (1962) Act of the inter-relation of the railways with other forms of transport and of economic and environmental needs, whether national or regional'.

The Government's first priority was to determine the size and shape of the basic route system for both commercial and social needs; the published map showed 11,000 route miles, and it was

Above right:
While Labour published the 'Network for Development', this did not preclude closure of some little-used parts of the system still in existence. Cairnie Junction is seen in 1967 with a Cravens DMU; the train had arrived from Elgin via the coast line and Tillynaught. The photographer was the only passenger.
G. G. M. Robinson

Right:
A two-car Derby Lightweight set on a typical service which came into the area of responsibility of the Passenger Transport Executive calls at Clifton Junction with the 11.12 Colne-Manchester Victoria. The northern end of the service ran outside the PTE area, giving rise to substantial difficulties later on.
John Clarke

intended that finance would be made available to sustain this network. For the first time, services requiring long-term financial assistance were to be identified and separately costed so that the Minister could decide whether grant-aid should be paid. A separate grant was to be paid for a few years to rid the system of excess capacity. Network stability was seen as essential if management and staff were to concentrate on providing the best possible service to the public.

The continued railway deficit, then well over £100 million a year, had continued. Since 1963, manpower was down by 29%, and the numbers of stations, locomotives and wagons by 44%, 45% and 36%. Traffic declined only marginally, yet the annual savings of £115 million were largely offset by a £95 million increase in the bill for wages and other costs. The 1962 Act's expectation of break-even in five years were thus incapable of achievement, and the Government accepted that part of the capital debt should be written off. The result of the financial measures was to be the ending of deficit grants as such.

In the provincial conurbations, the Government saw a distinct and urgent need for the integrated planning and operation of all public transport services. Their solution was the setting up of local Conurbation (later Passenger) Transport Authorities to cover not only the cities themselves but the areas around from which people travelled for work, shopping and pleasure. It was recognised that suburban rail services played a substantial part in the passenger movements in these areas, and full integration with the buses was sought. Agreements would be made by the Executives with BR on service levels and fares policies, and they would also provide grants. Wide-ranging alternatives would be permissible, and it was specifically suggested that stimulating rail travel by fares concessions, which had the result of adding to the financial losses on the rail services, would be quite acceptable so long as it was carried out as part of a comprehensive plan.

These, and other legislative changes, became law as the Transport Act, 1968.

Below:
Only social reasons could justify the continuation of the seasonally peaked service on the Cambrian Coast, whose other principal traffic was (and is) schoolchildren. The 08.12 Machynlleth-Barmouth descends to Fairbourne on 13 June 1967. *Stanley Creer*

Bournemouth Electrification

The completion of the Waterloo-Bournemouth electrification in July enabled steam traction to be eliminated on the Southern Region. Put another way, 150,000 tons of coal consumption were replaced by the use of 79 million units of electricity each year. Designed to be provided on the cheap, the scheme was notable for the use of push-pull operation on a large scale in Britain, and the refurbishment of existing stock for the new service rather than building new.

In the aftermath of the cost overruns of the West Coast electrification, it was only natural that a jaundiced eye should be turned on further schemes. Yet paring down the proposals to what could be justified economically, after taking population trends into account, and given the existence of the third rail for the first 29½ miles of the 108 from Waterloo to Bournemouth, enabled the scheme to be authorised in 1964. With the decision not to electrify beyond Bournemouth, some means of continuing the Weymouth link had to be devised. The Southern was already experimenting with push-pull operation utilising former 6-PUL/6-PAN multiple-unit vehicles, with traction motors removed, and a Type 3 diesel on peak hour Oxted services. This appeared to be the ideal method, using a high powered unit to propel trailers to Bournemouth, and with the trailers to be taken on from there with diesel haulage. Before adoption, the Inspecting Officer of Railways had to be satisfied, but trials held at speeds up to 100mph on the Tonbridge-Ashford straight proved that operation was straightforward, and push-pull throughout the Southern was agreed without demur.

For the main line services, 11 4-REP units, later augmented to 15, were fitted with four traction motors apiece, giving a nominal rating of 3,200hp. This was sufficient to propel either one or two 4-TC trailer units. The same control system was applicable to the Type 3 diesels and the electro-diesel locomotives, giving great

Below:
Less than a year to go before withdrawal, the up 'Bournemouth Belle' is pictured climbing Beaulieu Road bank in the New Forest headed by 'West Country' rebuilt Pacific No 34026 *Yes Tor* on 16 August 1966.
John H. Bird

Left:
Local services were provided by the 4-VEP units with 3+2 seating each side of a central gangway. Holidaymakers join an up local train formed of unit No 7762, in all-blue livery, at Lyndhurst Road.
John Glover

flexibility in the event of traction or power supply failure. All except the pairs of motor coaches, built new at York, were conversions of the equivalent Mk 1 coaching stock. The Open Seconds forming the end vehicles in the trailer units were fitted with driving cabs, but otherwise the greatest change was in the TBFKs (Trailer Brake Firsts), which started life as CKs (Corridor Composites). Although retrimmed and panelled with Formica, the interiors were spartan. Remaining services were operated by the 4-VEP electric units.

A basic train service pattern was scheduled throughout the day from Waterloo:

- A fast train at 00.30 in even hours, calling at Southampton, Bournemouth, Poole, Wareham, Wool, Dorchester and Weymouth.
- A semi-fast every hour at 00.47 to Bournemouth, with extension to Weymouth in the hour when the fast was not running calling at all stations beyond Bournemouth.
- A slow service every hour at 00.43 to Bournemouth, with a portion detached at Brookwood for Alton.
- A train each hour at 00.13 with portions for Portsmouth and Basingstoke, dividing at Woking.

Left:
A 4-REP EMU No 3001 arrives at Basingstoke on the up line on 7 March 1967. These were the traction units, pushing and pulling up to eight trailers to and from Bournemouth. The austere nature of the all-blue livery may be seen.
D. E. Canning

The Ultimate Type 4?

It was somewhat surprising to find that British Rail, having purchased over 1,000 locomotives of six different types in the Type 4 power category since 1955, were prepared to countenance yet another new design. However, the standard Brush Type 4 was not without its problems, and attention turned to English Electric's Diesel Prototype 2 (DP2), one of the privately sponsored contenders for the main Type 4 orders and dating from 1961-62. This 2,700hp locomotive had been putting up an exemplary performance between Euston and Liverpool, and later on the East Coast main line. When a requirement arose for a stopgap locomotive for Crewe-Glasgow services until such time as electrification might be authorised and carried out, an order was placed for 50 machines.

Compared with the prototype, similarity was limited to the main power equipment and certain items of running gear. At BR request, they contained some additional and advanced technology, with automatic tractive effort control, dynamic braking, inertia filtration and slow speed control all fitted as standard. This had the result of making the production models more costly, more complex and, inevitably, more unreliable than their progenitor. They were equipped for electric train heating only.

Rather than purchase the locomotives outright, a leasing arrangement was entered into; the Type 4s carried a plate to the effect that they belonged to English Electric Leasings Ltd. To British Rail this offered the advantage of not tying up capital and spreading the cost of the locomotives over their working lives; it also gave tax advantages. For the owner, the capital expenditure could be set against tax allowance on depreciation. Both parties therefore were expected to benefit.

Below:
The English Electric Co's prototype No DP2 came to a sad end at Thirsk, when it collided with the derailed wagons of a cement train. The locomotive was removed to York MPD and was photographed there on 3 September 1967. The engine was recovered for use as spare for the new Type 4s then in course of delivery.
John Glover

Left:
First sight of No D400, resplendent in the new blue livery as it emerges from the Newton-le-Willows works of the manufacturer.
English Electric Co

Employed north of Crewe on the London Midland Region, the class quickly proved their capability. Cecil J. Allen waxed lyrical about their performance when he recorded a non-stop run from Carlisle to Crewe with the up 'Royal Scot' in their early days. With an 11min late start, the 420-ton train pulled into Crewe, 141 miles distant, in just under 132min and 13½min early. This timing was equated to 127½min net of delays. At that time, the scheduled allowance was a not very demanding 156min, part of an overall Glasgow-Euston timing for the 'Royal Scot' of 6hr 35min, including the locomotive change at Crewe.

Although wired for working in multiple for up to three at a time, only the first two locomotives were originally fitted with jumper cables. They were all painted in the Rail Blue livery from new, the first diesel locomotive class ever to be thus treated.

Below:
An unidentified member of the class crosses the River Lune at Lancaster early in 1968 under clear signals. The locomotive will have taken over from an electric at Crewe, and the class secured much needed improvements to schedules on the route. *John Glover*

Salisbury-Exeter Singling

If economies were to be made, it was no good just talking about it. With closure not a realistic option, how was the Western Region to set about a cost-reduction exercise? After the closure of the branches, the WR was left with an 84-mile double track main line, with one intermediate junction at Yeovil for Weymouth and Castle Cary/Westbury. Intermediate stations were down to nine, and the passenger service redesigned to cover two requirements only: a direct service between the southern counties and Exeter, with onward connections to other parts of Devon and Cornwall, and a direct Waterloo-north Dorset/east Devon link, which traditionally produced the most lucrative traffic. The Brighton-Exeter through train was retained to provide the former, but the main service was to link the remaining railheads between Salisbury and Exeter with the fastest possible diesel-hauled express service running at two-hourly intervals. These were to be through trains to and from London Waterloo, calling also at Woking and Basingstoke.

The service pattern devised reduced train mileage to half of what it had been five years earlier, and single tracking was therefore a starter in making the whole viable. Features of the plan implemented on 10 July were:

- Singling between Wilton South and Pinhoe, but retaining passing loops at Gillingham, Chard Junction and Honiton. Six miles of double track kept between Templecombe and Sherborne to enable trains to pass at speed.
- Installation of tokenless block which avoids stopping for token exchange.

Right:
A pair of the Southern's Type 3 diesels Nos D6575 and D6563 approach Buckhorn Weston tunnel on the now singled route with the 08.50 Brighton-Exeter through train.
Ivo Peters

Top:
'Warship' No D812 *The Royal Naval Reserve* passes Battledown west of Basingstoke and takes the West of England route with the 11.00 Waterloo-Exeter. Double track was retained from here to Salisbury. On the right, a BRCW Type 3 takes the Bournemouth line with a freight. *P. J. Lynch*

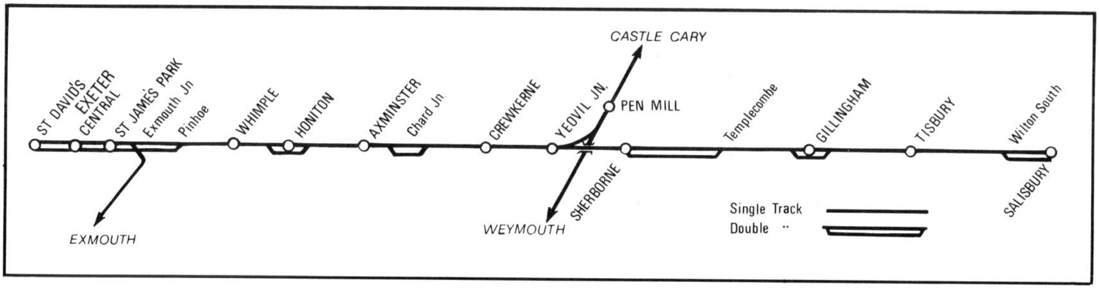

- Level crossing modernisation.
- Fastest-ever average journey times between stations other than for London-Exeter throughout journeys.

If the above were to result in such an apparently reasonable service, what cause was there to worry? First, while the *average* journey times may have been improved, if only marginally in some cases, the previous *fastest* times over the longest distances were much extended. Secondly, to pare costs right down, all the frills were removed and the few local stopping services abandoned. Local passengers had to rely on the main line service. This posed some severe problems between Honiton and Exeter, particularly for schoolchildren. But perhaps the most crucial element was the precision with which the timetable needed to be worked if a reliable train service was to be achieved. Whether it was the reliability of the 'Warship' diesels, delays on Southern metals nearer London, or failures in the signalling, the penalty in terms of disruption would be significantly greater than if double track had been retained. Unhappily, too many of the fears were realised, not helped by a rash of failures during the summer on the diesels.

Paddington's reply to criticism was that what was offered was a lot better than the alternative — nothing. Whether any Government could ever have sanctioned such a closure is doubtful, and the apparently unresponsive mood of the railway won it few friends. But further attempts at large-scale singling were only pursued half-heartedly, and later on the Salisbury-Exeter route secured substantial reinstatement of both stations and track. Economy had clearly been taken too far for comfort.

1967

Right:
Electric services were extended to Birmingham and the Potteries on 5 March. Class AL5 No E3079 calls at Stoke-on-Trent with a Manchester Piccadilly-Euston train. Standard timing to London from Stoke was 1hr 58min.
John Glover

Below right:
Brake tenders were still a necessary part of the scene. These 35-ton vehicles were provided solely to give diesel locomotives sufficient stopping ability when hauling a train of unfitted wagons. BR/Sulzer Type 4 No D77 *Royal Irish Fusilier* has two brake tenders attached as it stands in Barrow Hill depot on 30 July 1967. *David Percival*

Below:
With the electric services finally into place, Birmingham New Street became the timetabling hub of the rail system. The North-East/South-West services were comprehensively revised. BR/Sulzer Type 4 No D154 descends the Lickey Incline with a Bristol-bound express.
John Glover

APPENDICES

Right:
The winter of 1967 saw the last in which steam was working commercial services on the railways. By then work was almost exclusively concentrated on freight in the north-west, with but 362 locomotives to perform the remaining tasks. Class 8F 2-8-0s Nos 48720 and 48775 double-head a Gowhole Sidings-Tunstead ICI works train near Dove Holes tunnel in Derbyshire on 27 January 1968. *Peter W. Thomas*

1 Railway Traffic, Operations and Staff 1958-1967

<table>
<tr><th></th><th>1958</th><th>1959</th><th>1960</th><th>1961</th><th>1962</th><th>1963</th><th>1964</th><th>1965</th><th>1966</th><th>1967</th></tr>
<tr><td>Passenger journeys Ordinary tickets (millions)</td><td>649.4</td><td>637.4</td><td>663.2</td><td>683.7</td><td>670.4</td><td>646.7</td><td>629.0</td><td>580.4</td><td>547.3</td><td>537.2</td></tr>
<tr><td>Early morning tickets (millions)</td><td>127.8</td><td>111.8</td><td>58.1</td><td>24.1</td><td>—</td><td>—</td><td>—</td><td>—</td><td>—</td><td>—</td></tr>
<tr><td>Season tickets (millions)</td><td>312.5</td><td>319.6</td><td>315.3</td><td>317.1</td><td>327.2</td><td>291.7</td><td>298.6</td><td>284.6</td><td>287.6</td><td>300.2</td></tr>
<tr><td>Total passenger journeys (millions)</td><td>1,089.8</td><td>1,068.8</td><td>1,036.7</td><td>1,025.0</td><td>997.7</td><td>938.4</td><td>927.6</td><td>865.1</td><td>835.0</td><td>837.4</td></tr>
<tr><td>of which, first class</td><td>21.8</td><td>22.5</td><td>21.0</td><td>19.7</td><td>18.2</td><td>16.9</td><td>16.8</td><td>15.7</td><td>15.5</td><td>16.2</td></tr>
<tr><td>second class</td><td>1,068.0</td><td>1,046.3</td><td>1,015.7</td><td>1,005.3</td><td>979.5</td><td>921.5</td><td>910.8</td><td>849.4</td><td>819.5</td><td>821.2</td></tr>
<tr><td>Passenger miles total (millions)</td><td>22,150</td><td>22,270</td><td>21,547</td><td>21,061</td><td>19,772</td><td>19,575</td><td>19,874</td><td>18,713</td><td>18,453</td><td>18,089</td></tr>
<tr><td>Average distance per passenger journey (miles)</td><td>20.3</td><td>20.8</td><td>20.8</td><td>20.6</td><td>20.4</td><td>20.9</td><td>21.4</td><td>21.6</td><td>22.1</td><td>21.6</td></tr>
<tr><td>Loaded train miles (coaching) (millions)</td><td>250</td><td>250</td><td>253</td><td>254</td><td>248</td><td>233</td><td>226</td><td>213</td><td>208</td><td>203</td></tr>
<tr><td>Traction hours in traffic (coaching) (millions)</td><td>19.7</td><td>19.0</td><td>18.7</td><td>18.1</td><td>16.9</td><td>15.9</td><td>14.7</td><td>13.4</td><td>12.4</td><td>11.3</td></tr>
<tr><td>Freight traffic (million tons)</td><td></td><td></td><td></td><td></td><td></td><td></td><td></td><td></td><td></td><td></td></tr>
<tr><td>Coal and coke</td><td>153.1</td><td>144.2</td><td>148.1</td><td>145.7</td><td>145.0</td><td>151.4</td><td>147.4</td><td>138.3</td><td>131.7</td><td>122.2</td></tr>
<tr><td>Iron and steel</td><td rowspan="2">89.6</td><td rowspan="2">89.7</td><td rowspan="2">100.4</td><td rowspan="2">92.5</td><td>37.1</td><td>39.3</td><td>45.9</td><td>46.0</td><td>38.8</td><td>35.7</td></tr>
<tr><td>Others</td><td>46.3</td><td>44.1</td><td>46.3</td><td>44.2</td><td>43.0</td><td>42.8</td></tr>
<tr><td>Total freight traffic (million tons)</td><td>242.9</td><td>234.0</td><td>248.5</td><td>238.2</td><td>228.4</td><td>234.9</td><td>239.6</td><td>228.5</td><td>213.5</td><td>200.7</td></tr>
<tr><td>Freight ton miles total (millions)</td><td>18,426</td><td>17,711</td><td>18,650</td><td>17,590</td><td>16,104</td><td>16,537</td><td>16,003</td><td>15,429</td><td>14,825</td><td>13,609</td></tr>
<tr><td>Loaded wagons forwarded (millions)</td><td>27.0</td><td>25.8</td><td>26.4</td><td>24.9</td><td>22.7</td><td>20.7</td><td>19.8</td><td>18.1</td><td>16.3</td><td>14.4</td></tr>
<tr><td>Average wagon load (tons)</td><td>9.7</td><td>9.8</td><td>10.1</td><td>10.2</td><td>10.6</td><td>12.9</td><td>13.5</td><td>13.9</td><td>14.3</td><td>15.2</td></tr>
<tr><td>Average length of haul (miles)</td><td>70.57</td><td>70.59</td><td>70.24</td><td>69.06</td><td>66.77</td><td>65.56</td><td>66.78</td><td>67.51</td><td>69.26</td><td>67.79</td></tr>
<tr><td>Loaded train miles (freight) (millions)</td><td>126</td><td>121</td><td>123</td><td>119</td><td>111</td><td>92</td><td>88</td><td>78</td><td>68</td><td>61</td></tr>
<tr><td>Traction hours in traffic (freight) (millions)</td><td>30.4</td><td>28.7</td><td>29.1</td><td>27.8</td><td>25.4</td><td>23.8</td><td>21.6</td><td>18.7</td><td>16.2</td><td>13.8</td></tr>
<tr><td>Staff numbers (end of year) (thousands)</td><td>550</td><td>519</td><td>515</td><td>502</td><td>476</td><td>440</td><td>399</td><td>365</td><td>339</td><td>318</td></tr>
</table>

Above right:
The bogie tank car of 100 tons gross became a reality in the late 1960s. A train of the wagons developed for carrying light petroleum products for Shell Mex and BP forms part of the 6,600 rail cars owned by that company.
Ian Allan Library

Right:
The longest lived of the Type 4 diesel contenders was the Brush-built *Falcon*, No D0280. Entering traffic in 1961, it is seen here in 1967 leaving Paddington with a South Wales train. It was eventually taken into BR stock as No D1200, the one and only member of Class 53.
G. G. M. Robinson

2 Railway Assets as at 1 January 1958-1968

	1958	*1959*	*1960*	*1961*	*1962*	*1963*	*1964*	*1965*	*1966*	*1967*	*1968*
Locomotives steam	16,959	16,108	14,457	13,276	11,691	8,767	7,050	4,973	2,987	1,689	362
diesel main line	27	109	426	842	1,285	1,673	2,051	2,458	2,811	2,975	2,988
diesel shunting	775	1,091	1,373	1,708	1,894	2,010	2,009	2,004	2,000	1,987	1,754
electric	71	72	85	135	158	178	194	198	277	340	341
gas turbine	1	1	1	—	—	—	—	—	—	—	—
Passenger carriages											
locomotive hauled	35,474	34,325	31,450	29,841	26,961	22,575	20,469	15,591	12,950	11,112	9,307
diesel multiple-unit	1,349	2,417	3,244	3,820	3,998	4,074	4,132	4,107	4,109	4,087	3,988
electric multiple-unit	5,004	5,261	5,843	6,430	6,890	6,958	6,997	6,980	7,148	7,293	7,492
Non-passenger carrying coaching vehicles	14,994	14,926	14,271	14,871	14,551	12,482	11,521	10,725	8,081	7.445	7,401
Freight vehicles											
merchandise	451,700	402,297	374,596	374,309	369,800	325,407	258,173	214,349	204,344	174,099	143,308
mineral	571,553	542,241	513,164	512,849	508,816	464,199	404,537	382,330	357,592	332,854	282,649
steel carrying } others	81,638	75,659	72,593	74,789	77,668						
steel carrying						52,221	41,901	37,384	34,887	32,149	30,428
others						20,813	17,555	16,019	14,175	12,320	10,238
containers	40,212	47,421	50,151	49,071	48,296	46,535	41,436	36,490	33,415	31,969	31,038
Total seats/berths in passenger carriages (thousands)	2,446	2,446	2,361	2,331	2,203	1,953	1,809	1,546	1,411	1,323	1,248
Total capacity of owned freight wagons (thousands tons)	15,846	14,982	14,265	14,339	14,348	13,198	11,348	10,369	9,818	8,990	7,766
Passenger stations	5,410	5,264	5,060	4,877	4,712	4,347	4,145	3,574	3,161	2,869	2,750
Route open for traffic (miles)	18,965	18,848	18,484	18,369	17,903	17,471	16,982	15,991	14,920	13,721	13,172
of which, electrified	1,007	1,008	1,118	1,264	1,388	1,560	1,588	1,652	1,793	1,904	2,004
Route open for passenger traffic (miles)	14,622	14,454	14,063	13,865	13,653	12,915	12,631	11,670	10,884	10,165	9,882